Pesos To Pennies

Pesos To Pennies

A Filipino Immigrant's Memoir

Gladys Starkey

Pinay Mom
Publishing
Omaha, Nebraska

PESOS TO PENNIES: A FILIPINO IMMIGRANT'S MEMOIR

For publishing inquiries, contact:
Pinay Mom Books
c/o Concierge Marketing
13518 L. Street
Omaha, NE 68137
(402) 884-5995

Paperback ISBN: 978-1-945505-20-1
Ebook ISBN: 978-1-945505-21-8

Cover design by Elsa Chiao
Publishing and Production by Concierge Marketing Inc.

Library of Congress Cataloging Number: 2017937838
Cataloging-in-Publication data on file with the publisher.

Printed in the USA

10 9 8 7 6 5 4 3 2 1

For Tim, Marie, and Olivia

Contents

Introduction

How'd you get over here?

This was a frequent question I got from strangers, from someone who stopped me in the grocery aisle, or from people I'd just met after I told them I was from the Philippines. They often wondered if I met my American husband from the military. I was working as a call center agent in Manila when I answered a call from an American customer who was complaining about his satellite service bill. I called him back, and we talked every day. In less than a year, I married that American customer in my hometown, Daet, Camarines Norte, in June of 2008. I came over to America in spring of 2009 with one suitcase in hand. Leaving my family back home was a bittersweet decision. There was a feeling of joy and excitement, and my heart was full of hope when I saw America from the sky. Yet, my heart was filled with worries about living with my husband whom I didn't know really well. A lot of things have happened to me since the first day I set foot in my new country. I became a mother to two daughters, learned how to drive, ate a steak for the first time, worked four different jobs, and now, I'm pursuing my dream. I'm sharing all these experiences I've had with the people who are unfamiliar to a Filipino immigrant's story.

This is my memoir.

Call Center

"Gladys, take calls; it's queuing!" my call center supervisor, Liza, commanded. I had just pushed the button on my computer screen that made myself unavailable to receive incoming calls. When my supervisor said the word *queuing*, it meant I had to hurry up because a lot of American callers were waiting on the line. Some of them got impatient and annoyed and some of them would demand to talk to a supervisor or someone in the U.S. if they recognized a foreign accent.

I'd been working at the call center for a year; I knew that the average handling time (AHT) should be short so that the toll-free number was not queueing, and yet, I had still been on the phone for half an hour. The customer was disputing all the fees on his satellite service bill because he hadn't been properly informed about the additional charges for having extra television, a DVR (digital video recorder), and high definition TV. He wanted to cancel his contract, but got mad after I told him the cancellation fee.

"It's not my fault," he insisted.

I know it's not your fault. It's the agent's fault for not disclosing all the fees.

I offered to waive those fees for a number of months, but he refused.

"I don't want to pay anything except for the charges I was told about when I was signing up. If everything was disclosed to me originally, then I wouldn't have signed up, and I wouldn't be on the phone with you right now." he said.

But what you're asking is something I can't offer to you.

He argued.

I rebutted.

He kept on arguing.

I kept on rebutting, until I told him I had to transfer his call to another department. I had to leave a detailed note on his file, and it would take a few minutes to finish it, which is why I pushed that button on my computer screen so no calls came in.

I told my supervisor, "As soon as I finish typing this note, I'll take calls. Promise."

Beep!

"Thank you for calling DISH Network. This is Gladys. How may I help you?"

"Oh, yeah, I have a question on my bill," the customer said on the other line.

"Can you verify your name and phone number, please?" I asked, while looking at the customer's account that automatically popped up on my computer screen.

"How can I help you, Mr. Starkey?" I asked after he verified his information.

"I just received my bill today and I noticed I was getting charged for HBO," Mr. Starkey started. "I switched to this company because I thought that was free," he continued.

At that time, DISH was offering a promotion on premium channels—HBO, Showtime, Starz, and Cinemax—that were supposedly free for three months.

This was an easy call—not as complicated as the previous call I'd just taken. If all new customers like Mr. Tim Starkey would spend a few minutes reading their billing statement, they wouldn't be calling. But that's the reason I sat in the small cubicle at the call center in Manila, taking almost a hundred phone calls a day.

"The first bill we sent you is good for two months, Mr. Starkey," I started explaining. "We bill you a month ahead, and, yes, you're getting those premium channels free. If you would look at your bill, you can see the adjustments we made for those channels."

"How can I cancel them after the promotional period?" he asked.

"Just give us a call back on this date," I answered.

"Oh, now I understand. Thank you!" Mr. Starkey said. "But I have another question."

"What is that, Mr. Starkey?" I asked while I was leaving a note on his account.

"Where are you located?" he asked.

I'd been asked this question a lot because of the obvious reason. Mr. Starkey recognized my Filipino accent. I'd been working on hiding my accent for a year, but from time to time customers like Mr. Starkey could still hear it, and usually they asked about our location. We no longer had to lie to every American caller about our location to avoid prolonging the call. Before, we were told to say, "We're in Colorado." Some believed it, while others would say, "No, you're not."

"We're located in the Philippines, Mr. Starkey." I gave the short answer. My supervisor could see from her computer if we were on the phone for too long, and she would tell us to watch our AHT. We had to keep our average handling time (AHT) short because, as my supervisor told us, "That's how this outsourcing business makes money. Don't beat around the bush; give the right and direct answer—period!"

"Are you in Cebu?" Mr. Starkey asked.

Why Cebu? I asked myself.

"No, we're in Manila," I answered.

"I used to date a Filipina from Cebu," he said.

"Oh," was all I could say.

"So, do you have black hair?" he asked. I could tell he was smiling.

What the heck, Mr. Starkey? I wanted to say, but I bit my tongue. If he used to date a Filipina from Cebu, I was guessing he'd been there before, and I was sure he'd seen what every Filipino looked like. It wasn't like the U.S. where there were blonde, brown hair, black hair, or redheads.

"Yes, I do have black hair, Mr. Starkey," I answered.

"And brown skin?" he continued asking.

This was getting weird. First of all, no one had ever asked me about my hair and skin color. A few customers had asked about the beaches, the cost of living, the weather, if the Philippines is close to Australia, etc., but never personal questions.

"Yes, I do," I answered, "Is there anything I can help you with, Mr. Starkey?"

"Are you single?" I didn't know how to answer. I just smiled.

"What's your phone number?" he asked.

"I'm sorry, but we're not allowed to give that out," I said.

"So, can call me?" he asked. "You have my information in front of you, right? My address and my phone number?"

"I do, but is there anything I can help you with?" I asked once again, trying to end the call. We'd been talking for more than ten minutes.

He was insistent and asked me to read his phone number and address, so I did. He told me he would be home all day, expecting my call.

"So, are you going call me?" he asked in a very happy voice.

"I'll try," I said. Then we hung up. I was looking at my pen and paper on my small desk, which are odd because I have no use for them. The only time I brought a pen and a paper with me was when I was being trained on how to take calls and I needed to jot down some notes—that was a year ago, when I had just started this job. I wrote Mr. Starkey's phone number on the paper. Then another call came in.

⌒

Once I got home from working my graveyard shift (Philippines is thirteen hours ahead of American time) at the call center, I asked my younger sister Arianne to come with me to the drugstore. On the way, I told her about my conversation with Mr. Starkey and how he sounded nice and friendly. He wasn't upset or crabby like other customers.

Arianne didn't say much because she'd heard this kind of story before. But there was something telling me I had to call Mr. Starkey, so before Arianne and I went back home, we bought a phone card.

"Hello?" said the man on the line.

"Hi, Mr. Starkey. This is Gladys, the agent you talked to a few hours ago about your bill."

My voice was shaky, giving away that I was nervous. But I could tell he was surprised and happy to hear from me.

He said, "I can't believe you called. I was just about to leave and pick up the food I ordered."

He thanked me for calling him and he took my cellphone number right away, just in case we got disconnected, and we did.

From that day, he called me every day for an hour and he never missed a day. I learned he was from Morse Bluff, Nebraska. "It's a small town," he said. He was a truck driver, so he was gone all the time and drove to forty-eight states. He was divorced and had one child. He asked me to mail him a letter and a picture of myself, and said he would do the same.

A few weeks later, I told him the package I sent him was already at the UPS facility in Columbus, Nebraska. He didn't wait to get it delivered. He drove to the UPS store and picked it up. He said he was happy to see what I looked like.

Not too long after, I received his package in the mail. He sent me a card, a small photo album with pictures of himself, his child, his truck, his house, Hershey's candy bars, key chains, and a Mickey Mouse t-shirt that he bought while he was trucking.

I told my family and a coworker that I'd been talking to Tim for a while now. Some of them were happy. Some were surprised, while some were worried and warned me to be careful. I told them I thought Tim seemed like a nice guy; I could tell it in his voice. My coworker insisted that his voice and his phone calls every day were not enough reasons to say he's good. Even though we hadn't met in person yet, I was comfortable talking to Tim over the phone and I didn't have any doubt of his intentions.

It was in mid-September 2007 when I answered Tim's call at the call center, and in February, he wanted to come to Manila on Valentine's Day for a one-week visit.

I was feeling nervous, standing in the waiting area where I would meet Tim, who said he'd have on a Hawaiian shirt, a colorful one. We arrived at Ninoy Aquino International Airport half an hour before Tim's arrival time, nine o'clock at night. My sisters, Arianne and Con, and our mother, Mama, came with me. My mother came from Daet, my hometown, a ten-hour bus ride from Manila, because she was excited to see and meet Tim.

The security guard standing next to us wouldn't let us cross the street unless we saw the person we were waiting for. I lied to him. "Tim is already here," I said in Filipino, pointing my finger at the man who was pushing a big cart and had just come down from the airport ramp.

"Only two of you can go," the guard said in Filipino. I asked Mama to come with me while Arianne and Con stayed in the waiting area. The place was crowded with all the people arriving and their family or friends picking them up.

"Excuse me! Excuse me! Are you Tim Starkey?" I asked a guy who was pulling two black suitcases and wearing a Hawaiian shirt.

"No, I'm not," he said. I apologized to the man and I looked at my mother, feeling embarrassed for chasing him. He was not Tim; they just looked alike—the hair color, the body build, the kind of shirt that Tim said he'd be wearing. My mother and I stood there bumping shoulder to shoulder with the crowd, and I kept on looking at the ramp, waiting for Tim.

A few minutes later, I saw Tim coming down, pushing a big cart with his luggage and smiling at me. He was wearing a blue cap that said "Starkey Trucking" and a colorful Hawaiian shirt. He gave me a hug, and I introduced my mother to him. Tim gave my mother a hug and said, "It's nice to meet you!" My mother responded with a smile and said, "It's nice to meet you too." My mother practiced this line a million times.

We crossed the street where my sisters were waiting, and they were both happy to meet Tim. Con said she'd find a taxi cab to take us to our apartment where Tim would stay for the night. Then he'd go to the hotel we reserved for him the next day.

Our apartment was a two-story building with two bedrooms upstairs. When we got into our apartment, Tim asked me if he could take a shower while we dug through one of the suitcases he brought that was full of chocolates and USA t-shirts for all of us. He came out of the bathroom a few seconds later and told me the shower was not working.

"We don't use shower to take a bath." I said. I showed him how to use the dipper and a bucket of cold water, but he said he'd wait until tomorrow to take a shower when he gets to his hotel room. Tim slept in one bedroom while my sisters and I shared the other. Our mother slept downstairs, on a small mattress on the floor.

A one-week visit was too short for Tim and me to go to Daet so that he could meet my grandmother and my relatives. We decided to stay in Manila and spend time together with my family. In this short visit, Tim and I found out we had a lot in common. We both came from a big family. He has six sisters and two brothers. I have four sisters and two brothers.

Tim was raised in a small town. He likes kids and traveling. I'm a provincial girl, raised in a populated town with ninety-six thousand people, but it's still different from the city life in Manila.

Both of us have no father. Tim's father passed away when he was ten years old due to a heart problem. Mine is still alive, but I haven't seen him since he left us when I was six years old. My father took off with my then-seven-year-old brother, Jim, because he got an arrest warrant for threatening somebody.

A few days before Tim went back to the U.S., he proposed to me in front of my mother and sisters at the hotel on a beautiful morning. There was no engagement ring, party, or anything fancy except going to the restaurant right next to the hotel he was staying at.

My coworker—my only confidante at work—told me I'm crazy for saying yes to Tim, the man I just only met in person for the first time.

She asked, "Why are you trusting him so much?"

I told her, "Tim is kind."

My coworker just shook her head and said, "Well, if you're happy, I'm happy for you."

I'm not worried with my decision, even though it worries my aunt in Daet who did some Google searching about Tim. She found the same name with a bad record, but it's a good thing that's not the Tim Starkey who just proposed to me. After I told my family that I accepted Tim's marriage proposal, a few of them were worried for me. They believed that America's culture and beliefs were different from ours. I just assured them that Tim was one of the nicest people they would ever meet.

We set our wedding date for June 2008 in my hometown, Daet. My coworkers—except my confidante—didn't know that I was marrying Tim, the customer who called, complaining about his bill. I decided I'd rather keep the news to myself or it would spread like a wildfire, and I didn't know if it would be grounds for my job termination. I just told my supervisor that I would need a long vacation because of a "family emergency."

Our Wedding

Tim grew up as a Catholic, but converted to Methodist when he married his first wife. Now that he was marrying me, a Roman Catholic, he needed his old religion back because I had no plan to convert to another religion. My grandmother opposed the idea of me getting married in America. My family wanted to see me walk down the aisle at the Catholic church in Daet.

I told Tim we would need $3000 for our wedding to pay for everything—the food, his hotel room, the reception hall, all documents, wedding rings, flowers, souvenir items, rental for my wedding gown, his tuxedo, and bridesmaids' dresses. We were getting married at the beautiful Holy Trinity Cathedral at four o'clock on the last Saturday of June.

It would've been easier to get married at the courthouse, but my family wanted to see me get married at the church, not standing in front of a judge.

I didn't know getting married at the Catholic church required so much paperwork—the documents, seminars, a No Record Of Marriage certificate at the National Statistics office in Manila for me, while Tim, a divorced American, needed his divorce documents, baptism and confirmation certificates, and annulment verification from the Diocese in Lincoln, Nebraska. We moved our wedding date to another week because of all these documents.

Tim came over to Daet by himself, because his mother couldn't travel that far, and stayed for two weeks so that he could attend classes and seminars at the church, help me with our wedding preparations, and practice a wedding procession at the church. We also had to do our confession to the priest. I thought Tim didn't confess all of his sins.

"Why was your confession so quick if you haven't done confessions for years and years?" I asked.

"I don't have a lot of sins," he said.

The night before our wedding, my grandparents' house (where I used to live) was busy and full of people. There was a big tent in our front yard where music was being played, but no one was dancing. There was enough food for everybody, and a few guys drinking beer. They asked Tim to come and join them, but Tim only had one beer, then he walked around watching my family members who were cooking the food for the reception the next day. There was a long table for people who were chopping, dicing, and slicing pork and chicken. Tim watched them and asked questions about everything, including the three pig heads that were hanging on hooks outside the doorway. I told him those pig heads would be roasted and served at the reception on our wedding sponsors' and our tables. Tim just nodded, but I could tell he was still wondering.

That night, we had dinner with everybody. We served fried chicken and the famous *dinuguan*, a local delicacy of a pork blood stew with meat, onions, and other seasonings in it that is usually eaten over white steamed rice. It has been one of my favorite dishes since childhood. I asked Tim to eat some or at least try it. He firmly said no and ate fried chicken and rice instead.

After we had our supper, I went with my aunt to sleep at their house while Tim stayed at a hotel not far from our house. Superstitious beliefs are still popular in Daet, and they believe that a groom and a bride should not see each other or sleep together the night before their wedding because something bad might happen.

My wedding gown, Tim's suit, and the bridesmaids' dresses were all new and rented because I didn't want to spend a lot of money on those. I thought $3000 was too much for a wedding. Tim was paying for it, and I didn't want to ask for more money, so I made our wedding invitations, and Nanay, my grandmother, gave us one hog as a wedding gift.

In Filipino wedding tradition, the groom shoulders the wedding cost, but it has changed over time.

Sometimes, the bride chips in half of the amount or whatever she could afford to contribute. It all depends on what the groom and the bride agreed on.

I chose lavender for our wedding color because it is said to symbolizes love, devotion, and purity. My maid-of-honor, my oldest sister, Con, and each bridesmaid wore a beautiful knee-length lavender dress, while the groomsmen wore lavender t-shirts underneath the white Barong Tagalog, Filipino men's national costume.

Walking down the aisle was nerve-racking with all eyes on me. I was so happy, nervous, and worried that I didn't realize I was walking faster than I should have been. "Slowly," I heard our wedding videographer, on the side of the aisle, say in Filipino. I just couldn't wait to meet my mother and my uncle, who were waiting for me halfway down the aisle. I thought I would stumble, but I'm glad I met them without falling. I saw Tim in his American suit waiting for me at the altar, almost crying. He was standing next to my aunt who walked with him and stood as Tim's mom's proxy.

Tim and I solemnly listened to the priest officiate the Mass in English for Tim to understand. Our Filipino wedding was different from Tim's first wedding. At our wedding ceremony, a veil was put over my head and Tim's shoulders. After that, they put a white decorative silk cord over our shoulders.

"What's this all for?" Tim asked me quietly while we were both kneeling.

"For infinity," I answered.

Between the ceremony and taking pictures, our wedding lasted two hours.

They showered us with a mix of flowers and rice for a good married life when we were going out the church door. The reception hall was at the hotel, only a five-minute drive from the church. Once we got there, a few ladies waited for us at the door and gave us a spoonful of leche flan, a sweet custard-like dessert, which is for sweetness in our marriage.

We were expecting three hundred guests—my family members, distant relatives, friends, eight pairs of wedding sponsors, a dozen of bridesmaids and groomsmen. The reception hall's decoration was simple yet elegant. All the tables were covered with white cloth and there was a beautiful vase of flowers on each table. The three-layered white cake with real orchids sat on the table in front, next to the table where Tim and I sat. Tim was amazed to see the small white cage hanging in the corner with two doves inside.

He asked, again, "What's that for?"

I told him doves symbolize purity, and we would release them later. He just nodded and said, "That's cool," but his face was full of amazement with the number of people that were there and with all the food that was on every table.

We had three hogs, twenty-five chickens, a variety of seafood, and we cooked one sack of rice. Our wedding was a feast with different Filipino dishes.

After we ate, Tim and I went to every table and offered a glass of wine to every adult guest, and they put money in the basket I was holding. Then we released the two white doves inside the reception hall. Our wedding dance followed, and people pinned money on my gown or Tim's suit. He got more money than I did, so I took half of it after the dance. We asked our sponsors and guests not to bring any gifts because we wouldn't be able to use them in Daet. But we still got a few presents, like a set of plates, cups, saucers, and other kitchenware that I gave to my grandmother, my aunt, and my mother. We thanked everyone for their time and their gifts.

Before Tim went back to the United States, I recommended we visit a beautiful island, Puerto Galera, which is only two hours away from Manila. I had been there with my coworkers a year before. We rode a boat for two hours before we got to the island. On that boat, there was a little girl with long curly brown hair, and I could tell her father was a foreigner. Tim and I kept looking at this little girl because we knew our child would look like her—brown hair and light skin, if she would get Tim's traits.

The white-sand beach was beautiful. Tim liked it because there were a lot of foreigners there, a number of restaurants that served both Filipino and Western cuisine, bars, and boutiques where Tim bought a few keychains to give to his friends and families in Nebraska.

I went back to work at the call center without letting my coworkers—except my confidante—know that I'd become Mrs. Gladys Starkey. Tim still called me every day, even though I told him he doesn't need to, but he's insistent.

"I can't wait for you to come over to the U.S.," he told me.

⌒

A month later, our marriage certificate became available at the National Statistics Office in Manila, and we started processing my visa—a spousal or K3 visa. We were doing my immigration papers by ourselves. I read the U.S. Department of State website and different blog forums for a guide on filing my visa. Tim had a friend who helped him print and fill out forms. He gathered any documents needed before mailing the packet to the U.S. Citizenship Immigration Services. We could check our case status online, and I would let Tim know if he would be receiving something in the mail or if there was anything he needed to do.

My Immigration

Five months later, I received a letter from the U.S. Embassy saying I needed to set up a medical appointment prior to the interview date they gave me. We had to pay ₱10,000 ($200 U.S.) for my medical exam.

A few weeks later, I showed up for my interview with the consul at the U.S. embassy at Roxas Boulevard in Manila. The consul was so nice. He asked me how Tim and I met, how many times he visited me, when we got married and where, what Tim's address in the U.S. is, what he does for a living, and what I do for a living. The interview didn't take long. The U.S. consul told me to wait in the waiting area until they called my name to give more instructions.

A month later, I received a notice from the U.S. Citizenship Immigration Services saying my visa was approved. Tim booked my flight; I would be leaving for America on May 2, 2009, at 8:30 a.m. I gave my resignation at work, and a few weeks later, I received a yellow packet with all my documents, my Philippine passport, and medical records.

Before I could leave, I had to attend a pre-departure orientation seminar at the Commission on Filipino Overseas (CFO) in Manila. The purpose of the seminar was to prepare us for the new culture, beliefs, environment, and/or language, so we didn't seem ignorant once we arrived in our foreign destination.

There were twenty of us attending the seminar. I met fellow Filipinas who were fiancées or spouses moving to Australia, the U.S., Norway, the United Kingdom, and Canada. I talked to a lady who was also heading to the U.S. with a fiancée visa. She met her American boyfriend online, and he was still in Iraq, but heading back to the U.S. in a few weeks to meet and pick her up at the airport in Washington.

At the seminar, they showed us a video of a Filipina wife forced by her foreign husband to pose nude in the snow. "That could happen to you," the lady from CFO warned. "There are cases," the lady continued, "in which some Filipina wives are getting abused by their husbands, and we have to be aware with these—yelling, controlling behaviors are signs of an abuse."

After watching that video, she gave us a list of the Philippine embassies and consulates in the United States just in case some bad things happen. After the seminar, they put a sticker on each of our passports and gave us our certificates of completion. Tim was so happy when I told him I got everything done, and he said, "I can't wait to see you soon."

The night before my departure, I called my uncles and aunts to say goodbye to them. Two of my coworkers from the call center where I'd just quit came to visit me and said goodbye. One friend gave me a book about marriage.

We were all up at 4 a.m., preparing for me to leave. That early morning felt so heavy for me. My mother, my sisters Con, Arianne, and Charlotte, Nanay, my aunt Mama Josie and her husband, my cousin and her boyfriend took me to the airport—all in one van. At this early hour, the bustling city was so different. The traffic was moving fast, unlike what when the daylight hits.

Outside the Ninoy Aquino International Airport, it was crowded with different vehicles dropping off people like me who were leaving the country. We could hear the take-off sound of an airplane. I saw some fellow Filipinos giving their families hugs and crying.

Mama Josie gave me a small prayer booklet with the Blessed Virgin Mary on the cover and a light sweater with red, white, and black horizontal stripes. "For you to use when you feel cold in America," she said in our dialect.

Nanay asked me, "Did you bring your rosary?"

"I already have it in my purse."

I give my sisters a hug and said, "I promise to help you pay the bills."

A few days before I left, my sisters told me they were worried about being able to pay for the expenses at the apartment without me. All those years, Con and I had shared paying the rent, food, utilities, and our younger sisters' college tuition. Tim assured me he'd help my sisters by sending $300 every month. I told him I would get a job as soon as all my paperwork was ready, then I would send them money from my own paycheck.

I gave everybody a hug, then Nanay gave me a long hug. I could feel she was crying. "Don't fall for any temptation there," she said in our dialect, Bicol. I knew what Nanay meant. She was worried that I might meet someone in America and be tempted to leave Tim because she heard a few stories like that. "I won't," I promised her.

Between my friends and family, I got a lot of advice.

"Always pray."

"Take care."

"Call once you get to Nebraska."

"Don't get fat."

"Happy trip!"

I wanted to stay a little longer, but I had to go. It was my first time flying, and I didn't want to mess up, be late, or, worse, have the plane take off without me. All I had with me was my purse and a black suitcase that Tim gave me. I started walking to the airport gate. "Take care in Amerika!" I heard Nanay say. I looked back, trying to hold back my tears, and waved at them. They were all smiling and waving at me, but I could see that Nanay was still crying.

I showed the airport security guard my passport and itinerary, and they told me to put my luggage and purse on the conveyor belt. I had to walk through the door frame metal detector. My uncle, who used to be a flight crew member, warned me to hold my passport firmly and always keep an eye on my luggage because someone might steal it or put drugs or bullets in it.

I passed the security safely, and I was thankful for that. The airport personnel told me where I should go next. I had to stand in a long line to fill out a form and then pay a fee before I could find the airport gate I'd be taking off from. I followed where most people were heading. I had some time until my departure, so I found a vacant seat at the waiting area.

Some people around me were busy checking their phones, reading a book, drinking coffee, watching TV, or talking to another passenger. My phone rang, and I saw it was Tim.

"I'm calling to make sure you're okay and ready for your flight." he said.

"I'm nervous," I said. "It's my first time to fly and be out of the country, and I'm just by myself. After nine months of waiting and doing all the immigration paperwork—medical check-ups, seminars, interviews... I'm just ready to see you in less than twenty-four hours."

The flight crew attendants started calling passengers. They said, "First-class passengers board first, the elderly and passengers with young children next, and the last passengers to board are those with economy tickets." That included me.

When Tim was getting my ticket, I asked him to request a window seat for me because I wanted to look around when we were up in the sky. While I was waiting for the plane to take off, Mama Josie called me and said in our dialect, "We're leaving the airport now that we know you made it onto the airplane."

I looked outside and saw a lot of people inside the airport through the glass windows. Some of them were rushing and pulling their luggage. I saw parked airplanes, a few loading and unloading passengers, and one airplane on the runway, starting to take off. It didn't take long before we heard the pilot say that we had to buckle our seatbelts because we were leaving in a few minutes and tell us what time the plane would land at Narita Airport in Tokyo, Japan.

My ears started hurting while the plane was taking off. I couldn't hear well. My uncle told me to yawn, chew, swallow, or drink water during the take-off and the landing. I yawned many times, and it helped.

I could still see the ground, then a few minutes later, everything below got smaller and smaller. As I was in the air, I still couldn't believe that was happening to me. I had just turned twenty-three years old, and there I was, over thirty thousand feet up in the sky. All my life I'd seen people leaving our country because they got a job in the Middle East, Japan, or Hong Kong or immigrated somewhere. But there I was, heading to Nebraska, in the Midwest of America, to be with the man I just married last June.

The way the plane touched the clouds was unreal; I could see the blue sky clearly. A few people told me riding in an airplane was just like sitting on the couch at home, but to me, it was more than that. Literally, I felt like I was on the top of the world, seeing the clouds that close.

I thought about how my grandfather died without ever flying. Just like many people, he'd only seen what it was like to be in an airplane from movies or seeing a plane in the sky.

I remembered that during my childhood, my distant cousins and I used to play in the outfield, and we'd go crazy when we heard a noise from the sky—a helicopter. We'd jump up in the air, clap our excited little hands, and try to chase it as if we could make it stop. We would wave at it, hoping the pilot would see us closely and wave back at us. That was our simple joy of being a kid in Daet.

Now I'm here, riding in this flying object I said to myself. I know what a plane ride feels like.

"We will be in Tokyo in four hours," the pilot said. During the entire flight, all I did was take a nap, read a magazine, and look out the window to see the beautiful clouds.

Before I knew it, the pilot said, "We're landing in a few minutes; please fasten your seatbelts." Just like when we were taking off a few hours ago, my ears started hurting again, and I couldn't hear anything. *I think landing is worse than taking off,* I thought.

I was clueless about what to do next, so I kept reading signs and following other passengers that got off the plane. I was too nervous and embarrassed to ask anyone for help. But it wasn't that hard to find the gate for my next plane, and thankfully, I had ample time to find it.

Our layover time was three hours. I walked around the Narita airport and went to a couple stores where I saw a lot of Hello Kitty items, different kinds of chocolates, makeup kits, perfumes, and a whole lot more. There were restaurants, expensive boutiques, and shops where you could buy souvenirs and coffee mugs. I had a few U.S. dollar bills with me that I'd bought from a bank in Manila a week ago. Tim told me to make sure I had them with me just in case I wanted to buy something. I wasn't tempted to buy anything because, even though the amounts were in yen, I could tell they were all expensive.

I found a seat in the waiting area across from a family, sitting and eating food from McDonald's. I assumed they were Americans—white complexions, blue eyes, and blonde hair. I walked around, used the restroom, and read the departure board until the three-hour waiting time was over.

Back on the plane, I was seated with two Japanese ladies who were wearing medical face masks. I noticed the majority of the Japanese passengers were wearing them. I wondered why until I thought about the H1N1 virus that was going on.

I was happy to be in the window seat again to look around, and I talked with the Japanese lady next to me. She had a tourist visa to visit her Japanese boyfriend that attended school in Washington state. We talked about our countries and the city she was from, outside of Tokyo. We exchanged email addresses too.

Arriving in America

My ears were hurting again as the plane landed at St. Paul International Airport in Minneapolis, Minnesota, twelve hours later. I was looking out the window like a hawk, trying not to miss seeing anything below. *So, this is America, my new country and my new home from now on!*

I saw a few airport employees wearing orange safety vests, riding in a small cart outside; they were rushing to unload the baggage. The airport was so big, bigger than the airport in Manila. I followed where most passengers were heading and I was told by airport personnel that I had to fill out an I-9 form, an arrival/ departure record form, and stand in a specific queue. I gave my passport and the I-9 form to the customs officer, and he asked me to verify the information on my passport—my name, my birthday, and where I was heading. Then he told me where to go next.

I had to stand behind a mother and her young son that I assumed were Filipinos because of their features. The airport officer was asking the mother if they brought any plants, noodles, or chicharon (crispy pork rinds). She said no. Then it was my turn to answer the same questions. I answered no to all of them, but I wondered why they would ask if we brought any plants or chicharon.

In the massive airport, there was a lot of walking just to find my connecting flight to Omaha. *What was I thinking, wearing shoes with heels?* I asked myself.

Tim told me I would be riding in a "baby airplane" to Omaha, meaning it's smaller than the airplanes for international. From the sky in the baby airplane, I could see Omaha a few thousand feet away—the highways, houses, moving cars, tall buildings, trees, and fields where Tim said corn and beans would start growing in a couple months.

The baby plane started landing at Eppley Airfield, and I was happy and excited yet nervous. My thoughts started racing from *I won't be surprised if Tim is already here waiting for me. I know I'm going to like living here where I'll start a new life and hopefully a family someday. Although, I'm worried… What if our marriage doesn't work out? Would I go back to the Philippines? This is our first time living together as a couple, and we'll find out our differences, attitudes, and maybe temperaments.*

One of my relatives who's big on superstitious beliefs had warned me about Morse Bluff's area code number. They said, "The 402-666 is a devil sign." My relative believed that might be a warning for me and for our marriage, but I didn't listen to him. I didn't think an area code would affect someone's marriage. I was so hopeful that everything would work out and that Tim and I would get along so well.

Sure enough, Tim was standing in the waiting area holding a white teddy bear, red roses, and a small gift bag. We hugged, and he asked me how my flight was.

"I'm so happy to see you and I'm glad you made it here." he said. He told me that some of his friends didn't believe I was really coming over because his ex-Filipina girlfriend cancelled her plane ticket three times; that made his friends think I was Tim's imaginary wife from the Philippines.

Tim took my luggage, and we started heading to the airport's parking lot to find his 1999 white Grand Am. It was hot when I left Manila, but I felt chilly once we got outside the airport. Tim said, "It's not that cold!" But coming from the Philippines, a tropical country, the spring season was new to me.

"We'll be in Morse Bluff in an hour," Tim said while we drove out of the airport parking lot. We talked nonstop, and I couldn't resist looking outside. It was very clean and beautiful. No wild traffic, no peddlers, or kids begging for alms on the street like I normally saw in Manila. No noisy jeepneys (a public vehicle where passengers sit very close to each other) or tricycles (a motorcycle with a sidecar). No honking from any vehicle.

The roads were systematic and had beautiful surroundings. There were trees with different colors of leaves—red, pink, purple—standing so high. I was sure of the maple trees, but the other trees were unfamiliar to me.

"Are you hungry?" Tim asked me when we got outside of Omaha. "There's a Chinese restaurant at the mall in Fremont, which is only a few minutes away." He told me I could order rice or any food I wanted. I ordered rice and sweet and sour chicken for take-out, and Tim ordered the same. The smell of the food reminded me that I was already missing home.

Tim said, "We'll be in Morse Bluff in less than half an hour." I kept looking outside, trying to familiarize myself with this new place. I saw the big fields closely, and a pivot in the middle of one field.

"Is that a goat?" I asked Tim. I'd seen something cross the road after we passed a town called Ames.

"No, it's a deer." Tim said while laughing.

"It looks like a goat to me," I said. "And why do people let them run around on the highway? Who owns them, anyway?"

"Mother Nature," Tim answered.

This is my life now, I thought. *A lot of things will be new to me, like seeing cornfields in Nebraska when I've seen rice fields in the Philippines all my life.*

We passed a big golf course after driving over a railroad track, and Tim said, "We'll be in Morse Bluff in a few minutes."

Then we passed a river, and I told Tim it looked like a lake. As he was laughing, I saw a sign that said "Entering Saunders County," and another that said "Morse Bluff" with "128 population" written underneath.

"We're here," Tim said after he parked the car in front of the white garage. He'd sent me pictures of this house while I was still in the Philippines. Just from looking at the garage and the back door of the white house, it made me smile because, from that day, it would be my house too. It made me wonder what my days would look like while living here. Tim had been renting that house for a few years, and he promised me we'd buy a house someday. For some people the house looked small, but I liked it.

The house had many doors, and we used the back door, the third door, to get into the kitchen, which was small with hardwood floors and white walls. I could see the neighbor's house through the glass window.

The Hawaiian-theme decoration in the room greeted us. Tim said his friends did it for me. There was a small, round table covered with a white, plastic tablecloth with small shells on it. There were plastic garlands of different colors hanging on the ceiling, and my wedding picture was in a frame, sitting on the brown chest cabinet in the corner.

In that picture, I was holding a bouquet of beautiful white roses and smiling. But my face was so white that I looked like I was the first in line when powder showered from the sky. In the Philippines, they say having a lot of foundation on your face on your wedding day makes you look good in pictures; you become Miss Photogenic.

I grew up in a society that believes white is simply beautiful. A lot of Filipino brides-to-be try hard to lighten their skin with whitening soaps, whitening lotions, and even whitening pills before marching down the aisle. In other Southeast Asian countries, light skin equates beauty.

On the contrary, a lot of American brides spend money on tanning their skin—tanning beds, tanning lotion, tanning spray. I'd seen it in American movies and shows. To these brides, tan skin looks beautiful in contrast to a white wedding dress. It's interesting that I'm in a country where my brown skin is more appreciated and I don't have to use a lot of foundation to make my face look lighter.

Then we went to the living room, which has two big windows that are covered with white blinds. The big screen TV and stereo sitting on the glass table in the corner occupied a quarter of the room. I didn't see any decorations hanging on the walls except a large canvas print with a bear on it.

Tim showed me the master and the guest bedrooms, and in between those rooms was a small bathroom. He reminded me of a realtor because of how he was showing me the house. He asked me to come down to the basement with him. Once we got there, I whined, "It's cold in here."

He said, "It is not."

I told Tim that basements were not common to every home in the Philippines because we always got hit by typhoons.

He said, "Most homes here have one because it has a place to stock a lot of things."

I saw his washer and dryer in the corner, and just looking at them, I was thankful I wouldn't need to hand wash my clothes like in the Philippines.

I remembered when Nanay, used to tell us "Washers are only for lazy people. It doesn't clean clothes that good and it's expensive to have one too! So why have it?"

Well, I'll be a happy lazy person here in Morse Bluff for not having a back ache every time I finish washing my clothes with my hands, I thought.

We went back upstairs and out the front door where there was a "Welcome!" sign hanging on the door. Tim's neighbors were sitting on their porch. They'd been waiting for us to pull up in front of the house. Tim introduced me to Dale and Marge, and I asked them, "Did you make that sign for me? Tim doesn't know who did it." I thanked them when they said yes. I could tell they were nice people. Tim told me a little bit about them when he used to call me every day in the Philippines. I couldn't wait to know them well.

"Tim, why is it still bright out when it's already seven o'clock at night?" I asked. The sun was still up, which was weird to me.

"It's because of Daylight Saving Time," Tim answered. He explained that the clocks were moved one hour forward. I told him we'd never done that in the Philippines; it's always dark in there at this hour.

It seemed it would be a long night for me, but we let the night pass by watching boxing. Tim ordered a pay-per-view of the fight between our Filipino boxer, Manny Pacquiao, and a British boxer. Tim said, "Pacquiao is well-known in American sports."

"Why not?" I said. "Manny Pacquiao is as famous as God in the Philippines for bringing glory to our country."

I knew Tim was not a huge boxing fan, but he knew this was something I'd enjoy. For a lot of Americans, the chilly weather in May, having a basement, meeting neighbors, and Daylight Saving Time are not so much things to pay attention to, but these small things are part of the memories I won't forget about my first day in this country.

⌒

The following morning Tim woke me up at eight o'clock.

He said, "My sister, Sally, is stopping by because she wants to meet you."

We were both happy meeting each other for the first time. She asked how my flight went and if I liked being here. I said yes. We talked for a little while, but there were some words she said that I couldn't understand. The accent was what I had trouble with, just like when I talked to Dale and Marge for the first time and when Tim was saying something while we were watching boxing. I had to ask him a couple times, then he would say it again slowly. *If I could just put my face near theirs to understand them better, I would.*

Before Sally left, I gave her a pearl necklace that I brought from the Philippines. She was so happy and said, "I'll use it on my son's wedding day."

⌒

I called my family the next day to let them know I made it to Nebraska. The following days, I woke up late every morning and took long naps in the afternoon. My jet lag and the time change were hard for me. When I talked to my uncle on the phone about it, he told me to resist taking a nap in the afternoon, no matter how sleepy I was. "That's the only way your body can catch up," he said. I knew the transition would take at least a week or two, but I didn't expect it would be that hard.

My first few days, I also took long showers until no hot water was coming out. Tim asked, "Why are you taking so long?" even though he knew why.

I said, "Shower is something we never had while growing up. We always took a bath using a bucket of water and a dipper that you didn't know how to use when you came to visit me in the Philippines for the first time!"

Morse Bluff

Tim took a month off from trucking so we could spend time together. He took me to meet his family and friends and to other places he thought I'd enjoy. First, I met other neighbors that lived next door. He said, "Frank and Erma are a retired couple, and you will like them."

I asked, "Why did you have to call them first before coming over to their house when their house is only a few steps away from ours?"

He said, "I wanted to make sure they're home, not busy, and that it's okay to have company right now."

"We don't do that in the Philippines," I told him. "We just show up whenever we want to, and people won't think it's rude or anything for coming over to someone's house unannounced. Usually, you'll get invited to have a snack or lunch with them."

"Not here," he said.

When we got to their back-porch door to go in, I asked, "Do I have to leave my slippers outside before going into Frank and Erma's house?"

Tim told me to leave them on. Tim knocked, and Frank opened the door. I introduced myself to Frank and gave him a hug.

He told us to "Come on in," and we followed him, past their tiny kitchen. He led us to their living room where Erma was sitting on the couch. Erma said hi first to me, and I introduced myself, gave her a hug, and thanked her for the box of rice she gave me as a welcome gift. They asked me about my flight and a few things about the Philippines—the food we usually eat there, the kind of weather we get, my family, etc. Sometimes, Tim would pitch in and share his own experience from when he was there.

The couple told me they'd been living there for so long.

"I grew up in this town; it's a good small town," Frank said. "Morse Bluff used to be a booming town with a bank, two grocery stores, a lumber yard, a doctor's office, a village jail, a school, a candy store, a cafeteria, a drug store, and more population."

I thought back to when Tim and I drove around the town the other day. It was hard to imagine the places Frank was telling me about. I didn't see any of those except a couple businesses in downtown, one bar, one post office, grain bins, corn fields, and a few men wearing cowboy outfits.

Morse Bluff would be my new town, my new home, which was far different from Daet and Manila. No traffic, no pollution. All I could hear at night was a train sound. And in this town, I wouldn't see vehicles like jeepneys, tricycles, and buses like we had in the Philippines. I didn't see any mountains, waterfalls, beaches, or coconut trees either. There were no stop lights, only stop signs. I knew this would be a whole new world for me.

Tim told them about my question before we came into their house—if I should leave my slippers outside. I noticed both Erma and Frank had their shoes on. I wondered if they'd gone somewhere and just got home and that was why they were still wearing them.

I told Frank and Erma, "In the Philippines, we only put on our shoes if we're going to church, work, school, or at the party. We're always barefooted inside our house to keep the floor clean. I don't wear slippers or shoes inside our house here, and I'm not planning to."

Frank said, "That's what I noticed with Koreans too."

I found out Frank was a veteran of the Korean war. He got drafted in 1951 and stayed there until July 1953. I'd never heard much about the Korean War except some background when I took Asian history in high school in the Philippines. Asia, just like America, is rich in history because of its people, wars, cultures, beliefs, dynasties, etc.

"He has a purple heart," Tim chimed in.

"What is a purple heart?" I asked.

For Frank, Erma, or to some Americans, me asking this question might make them think I'm ignorant for not knowing what a purple heart is. It was something I'd never heard of, and I didn't think it was a purple heart in literal meaning.

"They give it to soldiers who got wounded at the battlefield," Tim explained.

Frank said, "I was shot in my left leg when we were exchanging gunfire with the North Korean Army."

"How did it happen?" I asked Frank.

"We were in the trench on the front line when an enemy came to the left side of the trench and started shooting us," Frank started telling his story. "The soldier on my left got hit and died, and that's when I got shot in my left leg, on my calf. Then they moved me to another division and took me out of the front line. I worked as a jeep driver—"

"And you know what, Gladys?" Erma interrupted. The three of us looked at Erma who said, "Frank went to Japan after that and chased Japanese girls." Frank was just smiling hearing that.

My late grandfather who passed away six years ago told me of his life during World War II when the Japanese invaded the Philippines. But unlike Frank, my grandfather never got drafted or served in the military. Instead he told me over and over again about their lives under Japanese occupation and the odd jobs he worked to support his family that he'd just started. He never had stories like Frank's who went to a war, got shot on the battlefield, and was now helping me to understand what a purple heart means. At the age of eighty-one, my grandfather died of pneumonia.

Before we left, Erma gave me a vanilla cake with white frosting to take home. They were both happy that we came over to visit. Frank walked us outside, and I asked "What's that door on the ground for?"

"A cellar," Frank answered. "That's where you store canned goods, and if there's a tornado, that's the safe place to go."

"Just like what they got in the movie *Twister*?" I asked, and both of them said yes.

Once we got home from Frank and Erma's house, Tim said he would take me to eat out since we didn't have any food in the refrigerator except a dozen eggs, bottles of water, and a six-pack of beer.

He said, "We're going to a restaurant that serves a good steak."

"I never had one before." I said.

"It's popular here in the Midwest," Tim said. "Do you want to try it?"

I said no.

The waitress started taking our order, and Tim ordered a steak. "Medium rare," he requested. I ordered fried chicken with mashed potato, and both of us had a glass of water. The waitress asked me, "What kind of dressing do you want for your salad."

I asked, "What are my choices?" I asked not because of the many choices she gave me, but because I simply had no idea what kind of dressing to put on a salad. I choose ranch dressing. I told Tim, "In the Philippines, salad is a dessert—macaroni salad, for example—that we eat after the meal. Not a mixture of lettuce, sliced cucumbers, a few cherry tomatoes, ring of onions, and a ranch dressing to eat as an appetizer. We believe appetizer or salad ruins appetite if we eat it before our meal."

The waitress brought our order, and I asked Tim, "How could you eat your steak like that? It's still red."

"It's a juice that makes the steak tastes good," he said, while pouring a steak sauce over it. "Some people eat steak rare, and they're juicier," he added.

I told him, "The next time we come back here, I'll order one, but I'll make sure it's well done." *I can't eat medium rare steak just like how Tim likes his or some people who eat rare for juicier steak,* I thought.

Tim said, "It's a Midwest thing."

I guess it's also a Midwest thing to put crackers in your soup, just like the couple next to us was doing. In the Philippines, we never ate soup with crackers, just soup.

The next time we went to a restaurant, I tried to have a steak, "Well done cooked." I didn't expect I would like it so much.

⌒

Tim and I went to Walmart to buy groceries the next day because I wanted to see food other than eggs in our refrigerator. I wondered how he did it all those years without groceries.

"I either went to the bar across the street or went somewhere to eat," he said.

I told him, "I can't do that all the time; I would get sick."

Walmart was a big store, and it seemed it had almost everything, from groceries to pharmacy. The store was different from the grocery stores in the Philippines—all toothpastes were in tubes, shampoos were in bottles, candies were in bags, coffees were not in packets, and I didn't see sachets that crowd the store's shelves in the Philippines. I saw a cake mix in a box, ready-made pizza dough, mashed potato mix in a box, etc.

We went to the Asian aisle where I saw different brands of soy sauce, noodles, and seasonings. It was interesting to see coconut milk in a can. I'd never seen one like that before. I bought one bottle of soy sauce, one bottle of vinegar, and bay leaves. We bought a five-pound bag of Jasmine rice. Then we went to the meat and produce department. At Daet Public Market, our vegetables, fruits, fish, crabs, and meat are always fresh. I'd never seen a frozen fish or shrimp in a package before.

We bought a pack of pork sirloin, breast chicken, a few vegetables, and fruits that would last for a week. I wanted to cook some Filipino dishes like our famous Adobo—pork or chicken meat marinated in soy sauce, and some stews. When we got home that day, I cooked a Filipino dish and steamed white rice, and I was glad Tim liked it.

⌒

The following days we visited Tim's friends, sisters, and his older brother in different towns, at least an hour drive from Morse Bluff. One of Tim's friends asked if I had another name in the Philippines because they knew some foreigners changed their names once they got to the U.S.

I said, "Gladys is the name given to me by my father. He told me he got my name from a character in a book he once read, but my mother insisted that she's the one who gave me this name. No matter what, I like this old western name that made some of my friends in the Philippines wonder how I got it."

I was happy to meet Tim's friends and relatives who became my friends and relatives too, but I wished I could have met my mother-in-law, Marie. She passed away six months after we got married. I remember the day when Tim called me and said his mom was gone. I never got a chance to see or meet my mother-in-law in person. We'd talked over the phone a couple times, and I could tell she sounded nice and funny. She sent me a letter when Tim came to visit me in the Philippines for the first time, and that was the only letter I got from her until she passed away.

⌒

Tim took me shopping so that I could buy some clothes. I didn't have enough clothes in the one suitcase I brought with me from the Philippines. Tim took me to the shopping mall in Lincoln, and when we got there, I didn't know what to think of the value on the price tags.

"Is a ten-dollar or twenty-dollar shirt expensive?" I still had no idea what the value of every dollar was there, but it was a good thing they were having a sale that day. I was surprised to see a lot of clothes, shoes, and pants that were made in China, Mexico, Vietnam, Nicaragua, or Bangladesh, and I'd seen some made in the Philippines.

Some Filipinos took pride in the clothes, shoes, underwear, and socks that were imported, rather than wearing items with a tag that said "Made in the Philippines." They preferred "Made in USA" tags because it symbolized social status. I remembered a friend in the Philippines whined when her sister, who lived in California, sent them clothes, all brand new, but they asked why they were "Made in China," not in the USA. If I told them that clothes that were made in China, Vietnam, Nicaragua, or the Philippines were cheaper than clothes or any items made in America, then they would understand and maybe stop whining.

I bought two pairs of white gloves, a stocking hat, and knee-high brown boots. They were also on sale, and Tim thought the prices were reasonable. But I didn't buy a coat because they were still on a high dollar—forty dollars at least. We saw a few garage sales while heading home, and Tim asked if I wanted to check it out. I was mesmerized to see what other people were trying to get rid of—books, photo albums, shirts, DVDs, shoes, toys, treadmill, pants,

Playboy magazines, you name it. There were clothes that still looked nice and barely used.

I bought long sleeve shirts and long pants that I could wear at home every day. I always whined to Tim that it was cold in the house, but he'd say, "Sixty-eight degrees is not that cold."

Wearing these warm clothes that I bought from the shopping mall and the garage sales will stop Tim and I from switching the thermostat, I thought. We ended up buying a bunch of things, and I told Tim, "I'm planning to send them to my family in the Philippines before Christmas."

⏝

I couldn't wait to attend my first Sunday morning Mass at the church in Morse Bluff, St. George Catholic Church. *I'll wear the new clothes we bought from the shopping mall*, I thought, so on Saturday evening, I asked Tim for his iron and iron board.

"Iron's down in the basement, in the closet," he said while he was watching TV. "But I don't have an iron board, never had one."

"You never had one?" I asked.

"I never iron my clothes," he admitted. I just shook my head, laid a blanket on bed, and ironed the clothes that we would wear for Mass.

When we got to St. George Catholic Church, there were already a few people sitting in the pews and a few more keep coming. This church was not as big as St. John the Baptist Church in downtown Daet or the

Daet Cathedral, where Tim and I got married. Those churches gave three to four Masses on Sundays and each pew was always filled up, which made some people stand at the back.

The Mass was about to start and there were still a lot of vacant pews. There was a man at the altar trying to light the candle using a long candle lighter, but every time he was about to leave, the light died down. "That's my friend Mike," Tim murmured to me while pointing to Mike at the altar, who was still trying to light the candle for the seventh time. Mike was heading back to his seat, and Tim said hi to Mike when he was passing our pew, and they shook hands. I knew Tim wanted to introduce me to him, but that would have to be later.

Then the priest came out from the door on the altar. There were two female altar servers behind him which I found different because I'd never seen female altar servers in any Catholic churches in the Philippines. We all stood up to sing for the entrance procession, but there was someone who was singing the hymn too loud, like a howling sound. It was coming from the back, and every time we had to sing, that person sang too loud, and he made noises sporadically.

The Mass was just the same as how we did it in the Philippines, except of course, not in Filipino, the peace be with you sign, and the way they do the Communion. But Tim said, "You should've went to the other way and followed the lady ahead of me to go back to our seat after you had Communion."

Instead, I went back against the people who were taking Communion and told them, "Excuse me! Excuse me!" They gave way to me, but I got confused and missed our pew.

I told him, "That's how we do it in the Philippines."

"Even missing a pew?" he asked.

Once we got home, I asked Tim, "Who was that person who sings loud at the church?"

"That's Mike's son, who is mentally-challenged," Tim said. "Mike drinks a lot, but goes to church every Sunday and from time to time reads the liturgy. They're good people."

That Sunday afternoon, Tim took me to St. Patrick Catholic Church in Fremont. He wanted me to see this church that was only built a few years ago. The church looked beautiful, new, and expensive. Our Catholic churches in the Philippines were big and old, like the St. John the Baptist Church in Daet, which was built four hundred years ago during the Spanish era. But one thing I noticed at the churches in Morse Bluff, I didn't see vendors of balloons, hand fans, candies, rosaries, flower garland, ice cream, or people begging for alms.

We went inside and we took some pictures where I stood near the beautiful stained-glass windows with the sun shining through. There were a few plants in pots of different kinds sitting on the floor. We took a couple more pictures outside. Then we went home.

⌒

The next day, we visited Tim's friend in Iowa who's also married to a Filipina. It was a long drive, but worth the travel because, for the first time, I met a fellow Filipina who'd been married to Tim's friend for five years. They lived out in the country, and she'd just started working at the nursing home a few months ago when she got her driver's license. She said she liked it here, and I was so happy to hear that from her.

We drove back to Omaha and ate at the China buffet restaurant. Then we went to the Asian Market. This was also Tim's first time to be at this store, where he asked a lot of questions every time he saw something new to him. I told him, "I'm buying a lot of products because who knows when we'll be back here again."

It was interesting to see what they had there—from imported Japanese chocolates to my favorite "cornicks" (toasted corn nuts) from the Philippines. I never would have thought that a smoked fish, anchovies, Filipino sweet sausage, cassava, and banana leaves in a package could be exported too. I bought a twenty-five-pound bag of Jasmine rice even though we still had some at home. I also bought white radish, water spinach, packets of seasoning mix, packs of noodles, banana ketchup, and quail eggs.

Tim wondered, "Do you really eat quail eggs in the Philippines; how do you eat it?"

I told him, "Just like how you eat the eggs in the refrigerator."

Once we got home, we had to use the big freezer to store all the fish and meat we'd just bought from the Asian Market. I cooked a lot of Filipino dishes the following days, and we would always have a plate of rice on the table. Tim liked some of my cooking, and some he wasn't really into it, like the fried tilapia. He asked, "Why do you cook it with the head on?"

"Because that's how we cook fish in the Philippines, and it's rare for us to cook them headless." I said.

⤳

The next few days, Tim and I stayed home, ate out once in a while, or walked around town for twenty minutes. He was not really that excited about going for walks because he thought people in town would laugh at him if they saw him walking. The postmaster told me that she'd never seen Tim walk before to pick up his mail, and that bothered me because our house was only a block away from the post office.

I loved to walk because that was part of my daily life growing up in Daet—we never owned a car. Walking was one of the things I could do every day in Morse Bluff, aside from watching TV, visiting Tim's friends or relatives, or calling my family in the Philippines. My family would ask a lot of questions about how Tim was treating me. I always answered that he was nice and had no temper at all. I didn't see any mean behavior from him. They were more surprised after I told them that Morse Bluff or Nebraska looked just like our province because a lot of people in the Philippines thought America was all about skyscrapers.

"Just imagine cornfields instead of rice fields with big tractors and combines, and instead of our public vehicles—jeepneys, tricycles—cars, pickups, trucks are on the road." I said.

My family also thought what happened to me when we went McDonald's was funny. I ordered the same food I used to order at McDonald's in Manila— "a cheeseburger, medium French fries, a small size soft drinks, and a spaghetti."

"We don't have spaghetti here," the crewmember said while looking at me like I said something wrong. I just ordered medium French fries, a cheeseburger, and a small drink instead. I told Tim, "It's weird they don't offer spaghetti here."

Tim said, "I think it's weird you have fried chicken and rice at McDonald's in the Philippines. And a delivery service too!"

"Really, they don't have spaghetti there?" my sister Con asked, speaking in our dialect.

"They don't, but McDonald's here is generous with soft drinks, napkins, and ketchup." I said.

At McDonald's or any restaurants in the Philippines, they didn't have soft drink fountains where customers could fill their cups as long as they wanted. They would just give you a couple napkins, packets of ketchup, and the size of your drink on a small tray, and if you wanted to refill your cup, they would charge you for it.

Before I got to Morse Bluff, Tim met another Filipina, Marla, in Fremont at the drugstore where she worked. He wanted me to meet her. I talked to Marla over the phone a few days after I arrived, and she invited us to come over to a Filipino get-together over Memorial Day weekend at the lake.

"You can meet me and the other Filipinas," she said. I promised her we would try to attend.

Before Memorial Day weekend, Tim wanted to buy me a ring. I left my gold wedding ring at the apartment in Manila, and I knew Tim was not really happy about it. We went to a jewelry store in Fremont, but I told him, "You really don't have to because I'm sure they're expensive, and my sister Arianne will keep my ring until we go back to the Philippines."

But Tim was insistent.

When we got into the jewelry store and started looking for my ring, I saw that was right. The rings—gold, silver, with or without rocks—were expensive. The saleslady asked Tim, "Does she speak English?" because it was Tim who kept talking to her. I could feel my face get red. I told the saleslady, "I do speak English."

I got nervous talking to her, and I didn't know why. I knew what to say, but I didn't know how to start. It seemed like those English words didn't want to come out of my mouth. The lady made me feel uncomfortable talking to her for whatever reason. We left the store without buying a ring and we went to the next jewelry store.

I'd seen one diamond ring that cost over $1000, while some rings cost more than what we paid for our wedding in the Philippines. I wondered why someone would spend that kind of money on something they just wear to show they're married. Tim bragged to his friends and family about how much our wedding cost in the Philippines, which to me, wasn't cheap at all.

It's true that most brides dream of a big wedding, but I thought $3000 was too much because I knew some couples in the Philippines who didn't even have enough money for their wedding, and were thankful enough just to get married. Some couples just waited until the local government or a Catholic church offered a free mass wedding.

Just by looking at the cost of these rings makes me want to throw up, I thought. We picked a simple ring with ten small diamonds around it, but it cost $400. We asked the saleslady if she could give us a discount, but she said, "We don't offer a discount; that's the bottom price."

I told Tim, "It's still expensive. Our gold wedding rings only cost us $300." But he insisted on buying it for me.

⌐

I hadn't even been in Morse Bluff for a month and I met a lot of Tim's friends. All of them were nice people, and they asked me a lot of questions, including my ability to speak good English. I wondered why they were surprised because a lot of Filipinos could speak English. I guess they were not aware that English is taught in every Philippine school from first grade until we graduate college, and as a matter of fact, English is influenced by Americans to Filipinos.

Permanent Residency

We filed the application to adjust my status to permanent residency and had to pay $1,070 ($985 filing fee and $85 for fingerprinting or biometrics). Once I got my permanent resident card, I could start looking for a job.

Before Tim's one-month vacation was over, we went to Spalding on Memorial Day to visit the graves of Tim's parents and his older brother. We stopped to pick up flowers at the market, and got on the road.

Tim said, "Spalding is almost a two-hour drive from Morse Bluff."

That was fine with me, because just like when Tim picked me up from the airport, we talked the whole way there. Tim told me more about his childhood living at the farm, his family, and some of his more vivid memories.

Tim's father had died when Tim was ten, and his older brother had died at a very young age because of an illness. Tim told me he had a rough life—not having parents around and losing a brother. I didn't know which one was harder—having parents that were completely gone or having a father that was never around.

I was six years old when our father left us—our mother, me, and my three sisters, Con, Arianne, and Charlotte. Our father left with our then-seven-year old brother, Jim. "He's the only boy to carry our name," our father reasoned. We didn't know if they would ever come back, or if we would ever see them again.

A year after he left, Arianne and I moved to our grandparents' house. I felt like a ball, bouncing back and forth, moving to my mother's, my aunt's, and my grandparents' houses in those years. We never saw or heard from our father; no phone calls or letters ever reached us.

My life was different from Tim's; he didn't have to worry about a lot of things that I worried about. I told him his life wasn't really as hard as he thought. But Tim said there was one tragic event that always makes him cry.

Their neighbor asked Tim and his brother to watch their three young children one night because they were going to a banquet. James, a seven-year-old, was one of the three boys. Tim told the parents, "James doesn't look well."

But the parents told them, "James will be fine."

Not too long after the parents left, Tim and his brother called them and asked them to pick up the kids because James had a high temperature. But the parents asked them to have James sit in the bath tub with warm water. A few hours later, the parents showed up to pick up the boys, and the next morning Tim heard sad news. James had died before dawn. The parents took him to the hospital a few hours after they'd picked the boys up that night. Tim said James's funeral was very hard. I could tell he was still affected by his death as he shared that story.

We pulled over at a cemetery near the road. This place was far different from our public cemeteries in the Philippines. Filipino's celebrate All Souls' and All Saints' Day, instead of Memorial Day, in the month of November. Every cemetery was always packed with people. There were candle lights on every tomb; people brought food; some played guitars; others offered novena prayers. My sisters and I would go around the cemetery and collect the melted candles, then sell them to a place at the cemetery that recycled them.

I didn't see any of those things here. I didn't see graves on top of each other making the entire cemetery look crowded—crowded with tombs. This place looked peaceful and the surroundings looked lively with artificial flowers on every headstone. If not for the sound of the flags flapping, the hum of the riding lawnmower in the distance, and a car driving through the cemetery, there would be silence.

Tim handed me the flowers we brought and led me to where his older brother and his parents were buried. He guessed that his sisters and brothers had visited before us, because there were artificial flowers already laying on the graves. We placed our flowers on each grave, and Tim asked if we could say the Our Father together. So, standing there together, we prayed.

"Why are you doing that?" I asked when Tim knelt with one leg in front of his mother's gravestone and put a quarter underneath the grass.

"Just to let them know I'm here," he answered, kneeling again in front of his brother's grave and placing another quarter. Then he did the same on his father's grave. Other people may have thought what Tim was doing was weird, but it was something I respected and understood, whether his deceased parents and brother would really know he was there or not.

Before we went home, Tim wanted to show me the house they used to live in. He grew up in Cedar Rapids, twenty-minutes away from Spalding, but when his father passed away, his mother, Marie, decided to move her nine children to Fremont, a town that Tim said he had never been to. Tim said a family friend told his mother that Fremont was a good town to live in. Tim was a junior high school student at that time and he would miss his friends.

That move was hard yet exciting for Tim and his siblings. Tim couldn't wait to see what life was waiting for them in Fremont, their new city. He was amazed the first day they arrived in Fremont, and seeing Omaha for the first time was mesmerizing for him—the car traffic, the buildings, the city lights, and everything was new to him.

Tim felt the same feeling I had the first time I'd been to Manila when I was six years old. I didn't know what to think the first time I saw McDonald's and Jollibee, a famous food chain restaurant in the Philippines. I'd only seen them on TV commercials. I didn't go back to Manila until I was fifteen years old to attend a seminar for non-government organization, and then five years later, after I graduated college in Daet, to find a job because there were not enough good paying jobs in my hometown. I also wanted to know what the big city life looked like—having coffee at Starbucks, riding the MRT (Manila Rail Transit), eating at nice restaurants, seeing local celebrities, or seeing things you would never see in Daet.

Cedar Rapids was also a small town. It was too quiet, and we only saw a few cars when we drove in downtown. "This is just like Morse Bluff except Cedar Rapids is far from everything," Tim said. "The closest Walmart is fifty miles away."

He remembered when his mother would drive sixty miles one way from Cedar Rapids to Grand Island to get groceries once a week. "The car and the trunk were always loaded," he said.

"Would you be interested in living here?" Tim asked. I said no. "I'm happy where we're at now.

I like Morse Bluff, a small town with only 128 people, yet we don't have to drive fifty miles to the closest Walmart."

We parked in front of a two-story yellow house with a big front and backyard. I didn't see any neighbors that lived close by. Tim's father was a farmer, and they used to own a big farm with a hundred head of cows, eighty sows, and they raised chickens for personal consumption. But when his father died, Tim and his brother learned how to run the big tractors for the first time and helped with the farming until his mother sold everything—the acres of farm, the animals, their house—so that they could move to Fremont.

Tim got out of the car and went to the front porch of the house to take a peek inside through the glass window. He came back and asked me if I wanted to see it.

I told him, "I'm worried someone might see us and think we're intruders."

He said, "We're fine."

The house was a neat-looking home, and Tim pointed to where they used to play when they were little. I was sure there were lots of memories overflowing in his mind and I was happy he was willing to share those memories with me.

⌒

I got a letter from the Immigration Services three weeks after we filed my application for permanent residency. It gave us a schedule for fingerprinting (biometrics) and instructions on what to bring and what items were prohibited when we got inside the building. We were not allowed to bring recording devices like cellphones or cameras.

There were three security guards at the Immigration Services building in Omaha. After we passed through the metal detector, one security guard told me where I had to go for my fingerprinting. I went to the receptionist and gave her my appointment letter and my Philippine passport as an identification. Then she asked me to have a seat until they called my name. There were less than ten of us sitting in the waiting area.

I was sure half of them had the appointment like me, and the rest were family members or friends accompanying them. I didn't wait long. A lady came out of the door from the reception area and called my name. Then she asked me to follow her. She asked me to verify my name, date of birth, and address. Then she asked me to stand on the wall so that she could take my picture. She started taking my fingerprints, left and right hand. The lady said, "We're done, and they will send a letter for your interview date."

Trucking

I'm happy that Tim took a month off for us to spend time together, meeting his friends and family and going to different places. I enjoyed our three-day stay at Montego Bay in West Wendover, Nevada. We went to different resorts in the city and ate at different restaurants and saw a lot of people. We also visited Mount Rushmore and saw the Badlands in South Dakota. I enjoyed that whole month with Tim.

He was going back on the road, where he'd be gone for a few days or at least a week at a time. I decided to go with him since I'd be staying home and couldn't go anywhere except to visit our neighbors. All I needed to do was sign a release of liability form from the company that leased his truck. I was excited to see the country—different states, people, some tourist attractions. Tim traveled the forty-eight states and he liked it. I'm not big on astrology, but they say Sagittarians love to travel, and I really do. I wanted to go places and tell myself I'd been to that place.

I started cleaning the truck sleeper while Tim was busy checking his truck. Inside the truck sleeper, Tim had a small TV, a few VHS tapes, and magazines. I found a black traveling bag on the floor that had Tim's clothes and other hygienic items in it. I changed the bedsheets and pillowcases and I started packing a few clothes, towels, toothbrush, toothpaste, shampoo, lotion, a pair of slippers, my laptop, a couple books, a journal, a bag of chips, and licorice.

"We're not going on a vacation," Tim reminded me when he saw what I packed.

"I'd rather bring all of these than run out of clean clothes and snacks over the road," I reasoned out. He just shook his head and put the traveling bag inside the truck.

Once we parked at the company's yard, Tim pointed out which trailer he'd be hauling—a big trailer full of farm gates and farm equipment with yellow straps all over. Tim delivered them to different store supplies around the country. He would deliver that shipment of farm equipment to three stores—two in South Dakota and one in Minot, North Dakota, which was a ten-hour road trip.

We walked inside the company building, and Tim introduced me to his co-workers—his dispatcher, the secretary, and his manager, who didn't look happy. The manager wanted Tim to go to Canada, not to South and North Dakota. Tim explained to his manager that he couldn't do that because I was going with him. "She doesn't have any document to show to the Canadian border officer." Tim said.

"Can't she stay home?" I heard the manager ask Tim.

The manager asked Tim to see his dispatcher and talk to him, but the dispatcher and Tim just looked at each other. The dispatcher just smiled and told Tim not to worry about the manager.

We headed to his truck, and Tim checked the trailer, making sure the straps were tight enough. He checked his paperwork, gave me the Atlas, and asked me to write the exits of the interstate and highways we passed. He knew where we were going, but he wanted to make sure he didn't miss the exit because "it's a headache when that happens," he said.

I was enjoying the ride, and it was amazing to see endless roads, cornfields, houses built in the middle of nowhere, and cattle in a big pasture. Tim asked me, "If we build a big house in the middle of that field, would you like it?" I told him no. Before I left for America, a friend told me that all I would see in the Midwest was land, and my friend got it right.

Sitting in the truck all day wasn't comfortable for my back or Tim's hips. We had to stop a few times at the rest area for a break and take a walk for a few minutes. We dropped off the deliveries at the two stores in South Dakota. Then we stopped for the night at the truck stop in a town only two hours away from Minot, North Dakota.

Tim said, "Minot is only a few hours away from the Canadian border."

I told him, "If I already had a green card, we could cross that border, take pictures, and tell everybody I've been to Canada, even though they say it's just like America." I promised myself I'd go there someday.

We had a sandwich and soft drinks for supper, then we took a shower afterwards. It was not comfortable sleeping inside the truck. There was not much room for Tim and me. One of us had to get up if we needed to use the restroom. Tim left the truck running overnight for air, but he shut it off a couple times and opened the small window in the sleeper.

We bought a donut and a cup of coffee for breakfast and ate it inside the truck. Then we started heading to Minot, North Dakota. We were both happy when we delivered all the equipment without any problems, and headed back to Nebraska. We stopped a couple times to eat, use the restroom, walk at the rest area, or fill up fuel, but Tim told me the fuel card that the company provided him was not working after he came back from the truck stop. He said the transaction was declined. It was past five o'clock in the afternoon, so he said he would just call the secretary tomorrow morning. We were done for the night and stayed at the truck stop in South Dakota.

I woke up to the sound of moving trucks outside, and Tim was already up, sitting on his seat, looking at the Atlas. I changed my clothes, brushed my hair, and grabbed my small maroon toiletry bag, and went inside the truck stop to use the restroom to brush my teeth and wash my face.

We bought a small bag of donuts, a cup of coffee for Tim, and juice for me for breakfast. We waited until it was eight o'clock so that Tim could call the company's secretary to find out why his fuel card was shut off. The secretary asked Tim if he got the Qualcomm message, the device hooked up to Tim's truck so the company could track where he was at and send and receive communication to their drivers.

"Oh, that's for me?" Tim asked, sounding surprised. We got a message yesterday saying, "Anyone who's suing the company needs to return the trailer and all the equipment ASAP."

"Someone just got fired," Tim commented after I read him the message.

"You just got terminated," the secretary said. "We got the packet from your attorney the other day saying you're suing us."

"I'm not suing the company," Tim insisted. But the secretary said the company decided to terminate him and to have the trailer and the equipment back as soon as possible.

Tim had an accident last January when he was delivering farm gates at one store in Illinois. He was standing on the trailer, guiding the guy in the forklift to unload the gates. But the guy missed the gates, and they all started rolling, which pushed Tim onto the ground, and the gates rolled onto him. There were twenty gates that fell on him and knocked him out.

"That was the time I'd seen stars around my head after I woke up," Tim recalled, and his dispatcher advised him to go ahead and drive back home. Tim forced himself to drive and see a doctor nearby. The doctor said he had a cracked hip. He wanted to sue the store where the accident happened, but instead his lawyer sued the company that was leasing his truck because he was an owner-operator and because of the Nebraska state law.

We dropped off the trailer and all the equipment at the company's yard, and once we got home Tim called a few trucking companies and some friends about getting a new trucking job. While he waited to hear from them, we stayed home together and visited friends and neighbors, and went other places, like a festival in Clarkson where there was a rodeo and a car show. I didn't know anything about rodeos or car shows, but "festival" sounded interesting.

Every year, we had a Pineapple Festival in Daet to celebrate St. John the Baptist's feast day. There was a colorful street parade, pineapple floats, creative costumes, dance competition, beauty contest, etc. But we didn't have car shows or rodeos like they have at the Czech Festival in Clarkson.

"The rodeo was yesterday" said a man in downtown Clarkson. Not feeling too disappointed, we decided to walk around to see classic cars at a car show. I could not recognize the car brands, types, or year those cars were made, but I was sure of the beetle car that we used to call a "turtle car" when we were little. We called it a "turtle car" because of its shape.

I asked Tim about the other cars. He pointed out corvettes, old mustangs, an old Ford, and a Willys jeep. I told him, "These old Ford and Willys jeeps are the reason why jeepneys in the Philippines exist. The Americans gave us all their used Ford and Willys jeeps they used during World War II when they fought the Japanese."

We took a picture of each car where I stood next to it and we walked to the church, which was not very far from the main street. We stood at the corner to watch the street parade where men, women, and some kids were wearing Czech costumes, and they were waving at the crowd. Some men in the parade were playing the accordion. Before we went home, we stopped at the bakery and bought a round pastry with red jelly in the middle. The lady said it's called a kolache. We had fun at the festival, even though we didn't get a chance to watch the rodeo. Seeing classic cars, the men and women in the parade, and eating my first kolache were things worth remembering from this festival.

⌒

Tim found another job where he would do the same, work as an owner-operator, except he'd be hauling different items or products to deliver in different parts of the country. In this new job, he would use a reefer and a van most of the time and haul an empty trailer once in a while. And just like before, I signed a release of liability form so that I could go on the road with him.

Our first trip was to pick up cheese cubes from Omaha and deliver them to Green Bay, Wisconsin. Once we got to the warehouse, Tim had a hard time backing the trailer into the loading dock. This was Tim's first time docking a trailer, and I had to get out of the truck to guide him. Just like a traffic enforcer, I used my hand to give Tim signals—if he was getting it right or not. I was embarrassed to see other drivers watching me on the street. We created traffic, and a couple times, Tim backed up and let the cars pass. Finally, Tim made it after a few attempts and he asked me to give him a high five for that.

Then we were headed to Iowa to pick up eggs and deliver them to the warehouse in Omaha, but they refused to unload the eggs. "They're warm," the unloading man said. Tim thought he set the temperature right, but obviously he didn't. Tim was getting frustrated; we'd been sitting in the truck for long time, and it was getting late. We'd gotten there in the late afternoon, and it was almost ten o'clock at night. Tim's dispatcher told him to go home but leave the trailer at this warehouse parking lot, set the temperature right, and let it cool; another driver would finish the load. Tim wanted to quit that night. "It's a nightmare," he whined, but he was happy that we were going back to Morse Bluff for a couple days off.

Then we headed to Denver, Colorado, to pick up jeans from a factory and take them to Cincinnati, Ohio. For some reason, I was just like a kid that couldn't wait to leave. I'd heard Colorado was a beautiful state where there were lot of pines and mountains. I was excited because, finally, I'd see mountains again, but I couldn't wait to go to Cincinnati either. I could see how these cities were different from the cities in Nebraska. It was a long ride, but I was happy to see some of the western parts of Nebraska.

And it was true; Colorado was a beautiful state. Its "Welcome to Colorful Colorado" sign manifested the entire state—the mountains, the pines, the skyscrapers, the trees with colorful leaves.

"Do you see that stadium?" Tim asked when we'd just gotten to Denver, he was pointing at the football stadium. I looked at the stadium that Tim was pointing at, and I told him, "It's so big. I'm not sure if that adjective describes its size. For me, it's humongous."

He asked if our stadiums in the Philippines were as big as that. I said no. Our stadiums were smaller than that, maybe because there was no football. Tim told me, "That's where the Denver Broncos play. It's a pro football team." I'd heard of that team's name before when I used to work at the call center. Some customers would ask on what channel they could watch a certain football game. I was familiar with a lot of football teams, but not the football game itself.

We passed three different states to get to Cincinnati, Ohio, and as usual, we stopped at the truck stop, ate, took a shower, slept in the truck, then got on the road again. Trucking for a week could be expensive. Tim didn't have a small refrigerator where we could stock food. Usually, we'd split our food. We'd buy glazed donuts and a cup of coffee for breakfast. There were nights we only ate a cup of noodles. That was the trucker's life, and I wasn't sure if that was something I could see myself doing for so long. But at that time, I enjoyed the experience, even if it meant sitting in the truck for many hours. I saw the beauty of America—the endless roads, prairies, wide fields, city lights in big cities.

Cincinnati was a big and beautiful city that made Omaha look like a baby city with its countless skyscrapers and different kinds of people. There were more African-American and Amish people. I didn't know anything about the Amish until I'd seen four boys walking out of McDonald's one morning, and they were all wearing the same outfit—the hats, pants, shirts, and suspenders. I asked Tim why, and he told me about them and what they're known for. Once I hooked up my internet at the truck stop, I searched on Google about the Amish, and I found them interesting. I didn't know there were still people like the Amish, who live that way despite the technological advancement the country has.

Our trucking days would look like this: go out east or west coast, rest for the night, deliver a load, pick up a load while heading back home, stay for a couple days, then head out on the road again. There were a lot of surprises and stresses sometimes, but Tim and I made every trip a fun one, even though he whined about all the hassles he had to go through. When we knew a certain trip meant a day off for both of us, we didn't complain, especially when we got to stay in a city like Las Vegas.

We'd just gotten done delivering a load in Provo, Utah, and there was an empty trailer that Tim had to pick up in Las Vegas. That day of the week happened to be our first-year wedding anniversary, and Tim asked his dispatcher if he could take a day off so that we could walk around the city. We were so happy when his dispatcher said yes.

I found it so interesting when we were a few hours outside of Las Vegas, that we saw nothing in the desert except cactuses and wild grasses. Then we passed that famous "Welcome to Fabulous Las Vegas" sign and saw the skyscrapers in the lively city. It was the last week of June, and too hot out. We wanted to stay at a hotel for a night instead of sleeping in the truck.

"Do you have an I.D.?" the guy at the front desk asked when we asked him how much it would be to book a room.

"I don't have it with me," I answered.

"Sorry we can't let you book a room today," he said firmly.

I told him, "I'm twenty-three years old. The only I.D. I have is my Philippine passport, and I left it in our house because I don't want to lose it. Just to think of the headache I will have to go through, it's better off to leave it at home."

The guy said, "Sorry. I can't let you book a room."

Tim and I left the hotel and went to the next one, but we got the same answer. There was no hotel room for us to stay in that night, and we had no choice but to sleep in the truck.

The next day, we walked around downtown like tourists. We took a few pictures and we went to a casino, but I was kicked out when a security guard came to me and asked for my I.D. "You look underage," the security guard said.

I told him I was old enough, but he asked for my I.D. again. I didn't want to argue with him, so we just left the place. We spent the day going to shopping malls, visiting wedding chapels, going to an all-you-can-eat restaurant, and walking around downtown Las Vegas, where I almost passed out. The heat in that city was hotter than Manila. It was too humid and too dry. There were no trees, just the concrete roads, tall buildings, and countless people walking, and I couldn't feel any fresh air. I didn't know why I blamed Tim for letting me walk that far. He asked me to go inside a fancy restaurant to sit down. The waitress gave me a glass of water, and she probably thought we were there to stay and eat, but we left a few minutes later after I finished drinking the whole glass of water.

Even though the front desk people at the hotel refused to let us book a room, I was kicked out of the casino, and I almost passed out on the street from the heat, our first-year wedding anniversary was still fun and unforgettable because I was with Tim in a beautiful city where I saw the luxurious hotels and casinos like MGM, Wynn, Riviera, Trump International, and Caesar's Palace for the first time. I enjoyed being there even though the street was too crowded and treeless.

꙳

I asked Tim to take me to the DMV (Department of Motor Vehicles) after we got home from trucking to Las Vegas. I wanted to apply for my state I.D. so that when people asked for my I.D., I had something to show to them. We decided to go to Lincoln since the Social Security Administration (SSA) office is there, so I could apply for my social security number too. I brought my unexpired I-94 form, my arrival/departure record, which was stapled on my Philippine passport, a magazine subscription that I'd signed up for, and a piece of mail for proof of address. The lady at DMV said it would take seven to ten business days before I got my card in the mail, but she gave me a paper card that was valid for thirty days.

Before we left the DMV, I took one copy of the driver's manual and I told Tim, "I'm getting my learner's permit soon before my I-94 form expires." It was only good for ninety days. If it expired, I wouldn't be able to use it as an identification, and I would have to wait longer until I got my permanent resident card. Then we went to the Social Security Administration office at the Centennial Mall.

Driving

I decided to stay home from Tim's next trip so that I could study the driver's manual. Tim was worried I might be scared or bored, not going anywhere while he was trucking. Our neighbors Dale and Marge told me to feel free to visit them anytime or call them if I need anything. I visited them once or twice and spent the other days studying the handbook at home.

There were a lot of things to know and to remember when I started reading every page. For someone like me who'd never driven a car, everything in the handbook was new and overflowing information. I now knew what those double solid or broken yellow lines on the center of the road meant. I also read about the rules of four-way, two-way, and all-way streets, which I found confusing.

Tim joked that I would fail the first time I took the test and he would call me a "loser" once I got out of the DMV. I promised him that was not happening because I was so determined to drive his car anytime soon. I took the practice test online over and over again until I got a perfect score. When Tim got back from trucking, we went to the DMV at the Saunders County Courthouse in Wahoo, which was at least a half an hour drive from Morse Bluff.

I was so happy that day because Tim couldn't call me a loser. I passed the test, and we went back to Morse Bluff with a paper learner's permit with me. Tim started teaching me how to drive that afternoon. We drove around downtown Morse Bluff for a few times, and I was thankful for Tim's patience. He taught me the basics, from how to turn on the car to how to run it. He never got mad if I messed up or got confused driving, rather, he told me "Don't get nervous. You're doing a great job."

The first time I drove to Fremont, I sounded like a broken recorder when I asked Tim, "Am I at the center of the road or am I getting too close to the shoulder?"

I was twenty-three years old when I first rode an airplane and drove a car. Growing up in Daet, I didn't see a lot of cars like they had in the U.S. or like those classic cars at the Czech Festival in Clarkson. In Daet, only families with money could afford a car because owning one meant you were on the upper social level.

My first car ride was when I was eighteen. Some Americans would laugh or feel sorry for me if they heard this, but not everyone had the same experience I had. Tim said, "Some American kids start driving at the age of fourteen because they have to." In the

Philippines, what a fourteen-year-old kid from a poor family could do was dream of riding in a car one day.

After getting my learner's permit, I always drove whenever Tim and I went somewhere, unless we were going to Omaha or Lincoln where the traffic terrified me. Driving on the highway for the first time was nerve-racking. I always adjusted the seat too close to the steering wheel so I could see the road closer. I would get nervous passing the curve on the highway and I always reduced my speed. I didn't care if some drivers got annoyed, impatient, or thought I was an old driver for driving that slow. A few cars passed me, but *they can pass me anytime they want,* I thought.

When we went to the bar across the street from our house one day, a guy asked me while laughing, "Can you see anything past the steering wheel?"

He said, "I saw you the other day driving and I wondered how you could still drive the car."

I told him, "That's why I have two small, red square pillows with "Huskers" written on them under my seat, to see anything past that steering wheel."

Even though I was not confident enough yet to drive on the highway, I'd had my learner's permit for a month, so I decided to test for my driver's license. Tim asked me to wait for a few more weeks until I was more comfortable, but I insisted I was ready. He'd been teaching me how to park the car, "The right way to park," he said. We'd been practicing at the Fire Department building in town, between two big rusty trash cans every afternoon. Parking was easy, except the parallel parking. Tim laughed every time I drove the car back and forth until I parked it right.

He also taught me how to back up the car without hitting or breaking anything, like I did when I was backing the car out of the garage. I broke the side mirror by hitting the side of the garage. I didn't know replacing it would cost $300, and I felt so sorry for doing this "accident."

We went back to the DMV in Wahoo to get my driver's license.

"If you want to pass your driving test the first time, a small town like Wahoo is a good place to take it because there are very few one-way, two-ways, four-ways, and all-way streets compared to what they have in Fremont. You won't get nervous and confused that way," Tim thought.

Tim had a friend who used to be a DMV examiner. "I get nervous when a Filipina takes a driving test because they're terrible drivers, especially in one-way or two-way streets," his friend criticized.

"Maybe because they're too nervous knowing it's their first time to drive a car and someone is judging their driving skills," I defended.

I passed the written exam and the eye test, and the DMV examiner and I headed to a car that was parked in front of the courthouse for a drive test. I buckled up first, and the examiner gave me directions on where to go and where to turn. I started the car and looked at the mirror, making sure no one was behind me, even though I didn't see any cars around.

I drove within the speed limit and followed the examiner's directions. I drove back to where we started, and then the examiner asked me to parallel park, which was not bad because I had the whole parking lot to myself. I parked in the first spot and backed up a couple times to make sure the car was not over the line or crooked. We stopped, and our seatbelts were still buckled. The examiner was writing something on the paper and she told me, "You have to work more on your parking, and you did good driving." She smiled and said, "Okay, you passed!"

"I'm a legal driver now," I told our neighbors, Dale, Marge, Frank and Erma. I felt like I'd made a great achievement that day when I got to tell this good news to them. I knew I still had a lot of things to learn when driving, like not turning the signal light on when I was still a quarter mile away. Tim asked me to turn it off, but I refused to do it. I feared a cop would see me and give me a ticket, and a ticket was not the first thing I wanted when I'd just gotten my driver's license. Tim just shook his head.

⤚

I'd been living in Morse Bluff for almost three months, and my days were all the same—go trucking with Tim or stay home. There were days I'd drive to Fremont to buy something or wash the car at the garage using a bucket of water and a rag. Our neighbor Dale saw me doing that and told me, "You should go to the car wash because it doesn't cost that much."

I promised him I'd do that next time. That night, I visited Dale and Marge and stayed at their house for a couple hours, listening to Dale's stories. I found out that Dale was also a Korean war veteran, just like Frank. Dale told stories about his time in South Korea and his life growing up. I liked listening to his stories and the way he said the word "anyhow" all the time. Anyhow meant Dale had another story to tell, and I was amused by it. If I spent a whole day listening to his stories, I could write a book about his entire life.

They asked me about my driving, then we told stories about driving, speeding tickets, and in that conversation, I noticed they said the words "a mile," "a half mile," and "a quarter mile." I also noticed that Tim said these words. I'd never heard him say "kilometer" like we did in the Philippines if we were talking about distance.

I also noticed that Americans said "pounds" instead of "kilos" and "north," "south," "east," or "west" when they gave directions. In the Philippines, we didn't have typical directions. We never told someone that the person's house was north, south, east, or west of another house or road; rather, we said the house was at the corner, or next to this store, or next to the big tree or we used our fingers to point it out. "Mile" was one word I decided to start using since I was already driving a car.

The more I drove, the less scared I felt. I could keep the 60-mph speed limit without reducing my speed when passing that curve on the highway. I could turn on the radio and search for a station while my left hand controlled the wheel. I could also answer a phone call and pass a car that was driving slower than sixty miles per hour.

One afternoon when I was heading home, Tim called me and asked where I was at.

I said, "I'll be home in fifteen minutes, but a slow truck with a tanker is holding up the traffic and I can't pass."

"I'm heading home too. I'm also on the highway, and I'm the one who's driving that slow truck with a tanker. I can see your car through my mirror," he said, laughing.

Even though I could do those things on the highway, there were a few things I still hadn't learned, like filling up the gas. Tim usually filled it up for me. In the Philippines, there were guys who filled up cars with gas, unlike the U.S. which was self-service. I tried to fill up on gas the other day, but suddenly I heard something from the intercom saying "It's a pre-pay." I had no idea what that meant. I just went inside the store, and the cashier explained to me how it worked.

Four-way stops were also something I still had to work on. A lady got mad at me when I didn't move right away when it was my turn during the four-way stop in Fremont. The lady threw her two hands up in the air, saying, "Come on, go!" If she only knew it was my first time on that road, and I got confused and nervous, maybe she wouldn't have been so impatient. In Morse Bluff, there were no confusing roads like that one, and people always waved at each other; they did not throw up their hands in the air like the lady in Fremont. That was what I liked about living in a small town.

⌒

Tim was home for the weekend and he asked me to wear something red—a Nebraska Cornhusker color—because we were having company that afternoon to watch the football game. That was my first time watching the game. "It's fun to watch this sport," Tim said. "Football is big, I mean really big, in Nebraska."

I didn't have a red shirt, but I had red pants with a small Huskers logo on them that Tim bought me from a garage sale. I just wore a white shirt with those. I didn't know anything about football, but I was happy we were hosting a little football party. We were having a pizza, chips, chicken hot wings, a vegetable tray, beer, and different pop drinks. Tim's friends showed up, and one of them asked me, "Do you play football in the Philippines?"

I said, "No because basketball is the popular sport in the Philippines. That's why Michael Jordan and Kobe Bryant are known to a lot of Filipinos."

He told me they're not big on watching basketball because, as Tim said, football was a huge sport in America. He also told me how some football fanatics bet on the games, some have season tickets, some watch every game. "And some are just simply a Husker fanatic who takes a week off when the football season starts, just like my brother," Tim said. I could tell there were a lot of die-hard fans around Nebraska, just by driving around Fremont where I saw Cornhusker flags hanging outside some of the houses or little flags on cars.

Watching how Tim and his friends got excited was more entertaining than watching the game itself. They were unhappy when the referee would throw a yellow flag against Nebraska, and they would whine for a few minutes. Tim stood up and asked everybody to give him a high-five when Nebraska got a touchdown. I asked him, "Is that really a big deal here?"

Tim said, "Hell yeah!" I heard them say a few times, "Go Big Red!" Tim's friend looked at me, shaking her head and said, "Welcome to Nebraska, Gladys!"

I thought I would be bored staying home just by myself, but I was not. Whenever Tim was home, we would go somewhere just to get me out of the house. On Labor Day weekend, we went to see his friend at the Fremont State Lakes. "He camps there every year," Tim said.

When we got there, I saw a lot of campers, tents, and people sitting on lounge chairs talking, smoking, drinking beer, or grilling. The place was packed. Tim said, "A lot of Americans camp on this holiday because of the long weekend." I met Tim's friend Chris who had a camper and a nice boat, and he let us ride on his boat. Chris let me sit in front and drive the boat while Tim was taking a picture of me. "This is the American life: camping, boating, and hanging out with friends," Tim said while Chris agreed.

When we got back home, Tim's friends called and said they were visiting and wanted to meet me. When I met them, Tim joked, "I'm happy she's here now because, finally, someone will treat me like a king."

"That's bullshit!" Tim's friend, Pam, exclaimed, laughing. "Don't listen to him, Gladys; we will train you like an American woman."

Like an American woman? I wondered what Pam meant by that. I'd been told it was a stereotype that an Asian wife, like me, was submissive. Based on what I'd read, some American men wanted to marry Asian women because of their "submissiveness." They thought Asian women just wanted to please their husbands and, just like Tim wanted, treat them like kings by cooking for them, doing chores, and obeying them all the time. I promised Pam I wouldn't let it happen and said, "Tim will never know how to be treated like a king." They all laughed.

✺

I still went trucking with Tim from time to time; we would go to new places or sometimes the same places again. In three months, we traveled to thirty-five states. We went to Maine and Maryland, which both had spectacular views, like a paradise. I also saw different states, passed long and scary roads, and saw how big America was. I was amazed to see the Phoenix Stadium in Arizona for the first time, then we got a chance to walk around Disneyland in Orlando after we delivered cases of bottled water to a warehouse in Tampa.

We also went to Washington, a state that seemed always busy, but I was surprised to see a homeless man on the street for the first time. The man was holding a sign that said he was homeless and had no money. Because of trucking, I saw interesting things or views all over the road. I saw how cars were transported and I even saw a trucker that almost lost his pants because he wasn't wearing suspenders or a belt. Even though that was unsightly, I would have rather seen that than a homeless man on the street. I didn't expect to see that in America, in a country that a lot of Filipinos thought had no poor or homeless people living on the street.

Although I didn't see all of the forty-eight states that Tim had been to, I was glad I'd been to different places and seen massive cornfields, pine trees, and mountains. We also met a driver at one truck stop in Washington who married a Filipina. The man asked us about the immigration process we went through and if it was costly or not.

He said, "My wife and young children are in the Philippines, and I go back there once a year during winter time."

We asked him if they were coming over to America, and he said no.

I told Tim I was getting bored of the trucking and I might stay home more often, since I had my driver's license. All I needed was my permanent resident card so that I could start looking for a job. In late August, I received a letter from the Immigration Services for my permanent residency interview. Tim made sure he was home that day so he could go with me to Omaha.

I was feeling nervous while sitting in front of the immigration officer, who looked serious, and he made smiling seem like the hardest thing to do in life. He had one thick white folder sitting on his desk, and I knew exactly what was in there—my birth certificate, our marriage certificate, other civil documents, our pictures together, including Tim's itineraries as evidence of our relationship, my medical records, the Affidavit of Support, like photocopies of Tim's vehicle titles, bank account statements, etc.

What we've gone through just to get over here is something I'm really proud of today, I thought.

The immigration officer started the interview by asking me to verify my name, my date of birth, and my address. He didn't beat around the bush when he said he would only give me a conditional status because of our age difference and where I came from. The immigration officer gave me two-year residency status and before that status expired, I would have to file for ten-year permanent resident status.

"I am protecting you," the immigration officer continued, while looking at Tim. I could feel the redness on my face when he said that. If I could have sunk to the ground or run away from his office,

I would've done that the moment he opened his mouth. Maybe that was the reason he didn't look so happy—or act very civil—from the beginning.

"There are a lot of foreign fiancées and spouses that only marry Americans to get a green card, especially women from the Philippines," the immigration officer continued as he looked at Tim then he turned his head to me. I didn't want to argue with his statement because he would probably deny my application. Maybe there was truth in what he said, and he'd seen it happen before, but saying that in general was not fair to all Filipinas, like me who had no intention of leaving Tim once I got my permanent resident card.

I showed him the piece of paper I brought with me. It was a document from the last call center I'd worked for in Manila, showing Tim was my sole beneficiary in my life insurance, not any single member of my family, not even my mother or my favorite sister, Arianne, but only Tim, my American husband, who this immigration officer said he's protecting.

The immigration officer took the paper from me and looked at it. He got up from his chair and he left the room and came back a few seconds later with another bond paper in his hand. He made a photocopy of the paper I'd given him and gave me my original copy. He sat down on his chair again and pulled two pieces of paper from the folder in front of him and he told me how I could remove my conditional status by filing a Form I-751. He said I could file ninety days before the expiration of my two-year permanent resident card. Then he asked me to sign it, saying I received a copy. He told me I would receive my permanent resident card in a few weeks.

Job Hunting

I went with Tim trucking to Georgia to pick up cases of soft drinks. Tim had to leave me at the truck stop so that I could take a shower while he went back to the warehouse because something was messed up with the delivery. He promised me it wouldn't take him long because the warehouse was not far. After I got done taking a shower, I sat down in the waiting area where there were a few truckers watching TV and some were reading magazines. A man who was holding a mop came up to me. I guessed he was in his late fifties, and he was wearing a gray collared t-shirt with his name and the truck stop's name written on the top left corner. He said, "If you don't mind me asking, where are you from?"

I told him, "I'm from the Philippines."

"That's what I thought," he said. "My ex-wife was also from the Philippines."

The man said he divorced her after he found out she was cheating on him. She told him the only reason she married him was to get a green card. The unhappy immigration officer's face popped up in my head. *So this is what he was talking about,* I thought.

"I'm sorry to hear that." I said, but I asked him not to think all women from the Philippines who married Americans were only here for a green card.

He said, "I understand that."

⬑

I received my permanent resident card in the mail in late September. Its expiration date was written on it. Having that card simply meant I could travel outside of the U.S., but I couldn't be gone longer than six months, because if I did, I might lose this permanent resident status. But I was so happy that I could legally work in America.

⬑

It was the last week of October, and Tim and I were heading home after we'd delivered a load somewhere in Iowa, and it was snowing. "It's unusual to have snow this early," Tim said. "Usually we don't get snow until the end of November or at least in the middle of December."

"I don't care what time of the year they get snow. I just want to see what a snow looks like." I said. I asked Tim to stop at the rest area where there are a couple trucks and cars that were parked. I got out of the truck without bothering to put my sweater on. I scooped up a handful of snow and showed it to Tim who was behind me, smiling. I was sure he was thinking I was like a little kid who got excited for a new toy. I just couldn't wait for the day when it kept on snowing so that I could wear my winter coat, boots, gloves, and stocking hat for the first time.

I posted pictures of the snow on Facebook so that my family and friends in the Philippines could see it. For a lot of Filipinos, seeing a snow meant your life was above ordinary. The manager at the last call center I worked for in Manila took her six-year-old daughter to California to see a snow for the first time. "It's a Christmas gift," our manager said. How lucky her young daughter was to have that kind of Christmas gift. The roundtrip ticket cost from Manila to California was four months of my salary working at the call center, and there was no guarantee if my tourist visa would have been approved or not.

Tim's cousin in Florida called him and said, "I saw on the news that this year Nebraska will have a bad winter; it's going to be nasty." I wasn't sure what kind of nasty winter Tim's cousin was talking about, but Tim said, "If it's bad, it means roads are closed, and there are cars in the ditch."

For the first time, Tim turned the heat on inside the house, after I'd been telling I felt cold despite the sweater, socks, and thick pants I was wearing. My lips and skin started getting dry. Tim told me I had to use a lip balm and put lotion on every day. I wasn't sure what my first winter would look like, but staying home most of the time was not a bad idea.

⤳

When we visited Tim's friend in Iowa who was married to a Filipina, she gave me a box that I could use if I wanted to send a few things to my family, and I started filling up that box right away. After a while, it was full, so I asked Tim to help me tape the big box while I was sitting on top of it. Someone picked the box up from our house, and I just had to pay him for the shipping fee to the Philippines.

I put a lot of things in this box—old blankets, picture frames, Tim's old shirts, clothes, purses, and shoes that we bought from the Goodwill and garage sales. I also sent bags of chocolates, boxes of cereals, cans of hot chocolate mix and coffee, and jars of peanut butter. I also put the hotel bar soaps, body lotion, and pads of sticky notes that our neighbor Marge gave me.

I made sure we had Christmas cards for my mother, my grandmother, my uncle, and my aunts with a dollar bill in them that made Tim asked why I'm doing it. I told him it's a souvenir which I knew my family wouldn't mind and they would be excited once they opened the box.

My uncle who worked in the Middle East used to send a box once a year, and we would get a bag of M&M's, a jar of peanut butter, coffee, and Hershey's candy bars. Nanay would count the candies in the bag, then divide them to all of us—herself, my sisters, and our grandfather. She would tell my sisters and I not to eat them all at once and to save some to take to school the next day so that we didn't spend our allowance.

My family was happy and excited after I told them about the box I sent them.

⤜

In mid-November, I found out I was pregnant with our first child and due in July. Some mothers waited until they were past the first trimester before sharing the news with everybody, but we couldn't wait to tell our family and friends about my pregnancy. I decided not to go trucking with Tim anymore because I didn't know what my pregnancy would feel like.

Suddenly, I was hesitant to look for a job, but the $300 we were sending to my family in the Philippines every month was the reason I had to submit a couple job applications online. Tim didn't say anything or complain about it, but it would be better if the money we were giving to my family was coming from me and my own hard work. Sending money to a family every month was not part of Tim's culture, or generally, the American culture. I also wanted to experience what it was like working with Americans. I wanted to meet more people and hopefully make friends with them.

I'd seen a work from home ad online where the main office was in Colorado, and I didn't think twice about sending an application. According to the job description, it was like having a home call center where I would be getting calls from people who had questions about their cellphone service account. This sounded exciting because a customer service job was something I was familiar with, and I would be saving money on gas by not driving. But I didn't finish my application because of the demanding requirements—a certain computer software, phone line, and countless paperwork.

The following week, I submitted another online application to one call center in Lincoln. I got a call from the hiring personnel a day later, and she told me about their business and how much I would get paid. We set up an interview, but I canceled it right away when Tim told me it was not worth the drive and that driving in winter was worse.

I applied to another call center, this time in Fremont, a half an hour drive. I went for an interview a few days later. I thought I understood and answered all the questions of the interviewing manager, and a supervisor gave me a quick tour of the building. This call center was small compared to the call centers in Manila where there were tons of agents working the graveyard shift, taking calls from Americans, Canadians, Australians, and the British. I only saw a few agents, and one agent was upset, explaining something to the customer on the other line. This scenario only brought back memories of the same job I had in Manila.

The supervisor told me the duties I would do if they offered me the job. She told me they would call me in two weeks to let me know if I got the job or not. Two weeks later, I didn't hear from them. I gave them a few more days, but I didn't get any call. So, I called them, but the secretary said they were still reviewing my application and would get back to me once they were done.

⌒

Tim stayed home for a few days for Thanksgiving. We celebrated Thanksgiving Day at his brother's and sister's houses, who both live in the same town. We had lunch at my sister-in-law's house first, then went to my brother-in-law's house for supper. Once we got to my sister-in-law's house, they were watching the movie *Band of Brothers* while my sister-in-law went back and forth in the kitchen, checking on the food she was cooking. I followed her in the kitchen and asked if she needed help. She said, "I'm almost done cooking; make yourself comfortable," but I insisted on standing next to her and watching her.

She prepared a lot of food. For me, it was a feast, and I wondered if Thanksgiving was the biggest holiday in the U.S. There were mashed potatoes with gravy, sweetcorn, dinner rolls, drinks, a pumpkin pie, and one big turkey. I'd never had turkey before because, in the Philippines, we ate pork, chicken, beef, fish, and seafood.

They asked if we celebrated Thanksgiving in the Philippines. I said we don't. "So, the pilgrims didn't stop at your country?" one relative asked.

"Unfortunately, they did not," I answered. "Christmas and New Year are big holidays in the Philippines, but we never celebrate Thanksgiving there."

The turkey tasted good, and I was full. I wasn't sure if I could still eat supper after this, and when we got to my brother-in-law's house, we had the same meal.

〜

It was the second week of December, and the snow kept falling. I felt like I was on the high moon sporting my winter outfit—knee-high brown boots, a pink coat, a black stocking hat, and white thick gloves. Tim and I walked to the post office to pick up the mail. He insisted that we could drive there, but I told him I wanted to walk so that he could take a picture of me outside with the snow as my background. It was amazing to see our breath when we talked, just like those actors I'd seen in American movies.

I stood in the middle of the road holding the mail we'd just gotten from the post office, and before we got inside our house, I wrote our names in the snow in the front lawn. I laid down on the side and I asked Tim to take a picture. I wanted my family to see these pictures on Facebook because I was sure they would all get excited once they did.

〜

I called the call center in Fremont once again, but the secretary told me to wait for a phone call because the management hadn't made a decision yet. Tim thought it would be better if I waited because winter was getting bad. He said, "I would worry more if you get the job right now and drive in snow, which you haven't done before."

"I'll just wait, I guess." I said.

﹎

It was Christmas, my favorite holiday, but there I was, without the same excitement I used to have when we celebrated this holiday in the Philippines. I was missing home. "It's crazy to think I've been living here for seven months now." I told Tim. "I didn't know what to expect the first day I arrived here, and now I'm speaking English every day and I've seen a snow for the first time."

The Christmas in America was not as festive as in the Philippines, where having a lot of food on the table and gifts under the Christmas tree were not the main thing. Family members who lived outside the town or the province would go back home for a few days to celebrate Christmas and New Year with their family. It was sad to say that was my first lonely Christmas, maybe because I was living halfway around the world from my family.

What we had in Morse Bluff were dancing Christmas lights hanging on the windows and a big Christmas tree that was standing tall in the corner next to our couch with a few presents underneath it to be given away to friends and Tim's relatives. No lanterns hanging outside or inside our house. No group of people outside the door, singing Christmas carols. No children knocking on our door to ask for money, and no people coming over to eat with us.

Our neighbors Dale and Marge invited us to come over to their house the day after Christmas. Marge made a chili soup and pineapple upside-down cake. Marge knew that pineapple was my favorite fruit to eat in the Philippines. She thought I would like it, and I did.

The New Year celebration was no different—just Tim and I and a pan of chocolate cake I'd baked. I didn't hear fireworks outside. No noise except a passing train or the sound of our TV, showing the New Year's countdown.

Our New Year's Eve in the Philippines was not like this. When the New Year arrived, we would clang pots and pans to make noise and leave the door wide open for good luck to come in. My grandmother always had twelve different round fruits on our dining table for good fortune, twelve fruits for twelve months. We always had noodles for long life, a sticky rice cake for good luck to stick the whole year, and we wore clothes or dresses with polka dots as a symbol of coins or money. These were beliefs that were influenced by Chinese people in the Philippines.

There was another belief that Arianne and I used to do when twelve o'clock arrived. We used to jump up and down many times because we heard you'd get taller when you did that, but obviously, that was not true because we were still short. Some Americans might have found all these beliefs comical and odd, but I would rather do all these and have a happy New Year than a lonely one. We didn't have food for good luck or for long life, no fireworks or noise happening outside our house in Morse Bluff. All I could see outside were inches of snow that were covering our entire surroundings, including trees, and making the outside look bright. Tim and I went to bed early on New Year's Eve.

⌐⌐

I called the call center again in Fremont, but to my dismay, the manager who interviewed me said their business had just filed bankruptcy, and I would have to apply somewhere else. "I'm so sorry for making you wait this long," he said. The following days, I looked for other jobs online and in the paper. Tim was right, I would have to wait until the winter was over because the next few weeks would be bad.

I couldn't leave the house because I was too scared to drive. I stayed home and hibernated for many days while Tim went trucking. Our neighbors, Dale, Marge, Frank, and Erma got worried when they hadn't seen me for a few days, and they called to see if I was okay. But I'd just spent my days at home watching TV, cooking, watching our neighbor Dale clear our sidewalk, and checking available jobs online.

∽

Soon, it was February, and I was thinking that if I started sending applications, the winter would be almost over once I got a job. I found a few job ads, but their qualifications were not applicable to me. That was the reason some Filipino immigrants took whatever job they could find, regardless of the educational background they had from the Philippines. The job qualifications and requirements were a challenge to many.

I didn't know what kind of job I could get here, or if I would ever get a job related to my college degree, Business Administration with an emphasis in Marketing. I was not sure if employers would consider my education from the Philippines or the call center experience I had. One of my aunts went to London for a vacation, and she had her transcript of records evaluated at a university there. Her master's degree in the Philippines didn't credit all the subjects she had in London. She said, "Basically, my master degree is only a college equivalent to that university." That meant my college degree would only be equivalent to a high school diploma here. I didn't have any office or clerical experience to work as a secretary or the background to work in sales or marketing.

I responded to an online ad that said, "No experience needed!" A truck stop in Fremont was looking for overnight help to clean their building. Tim was not excited after I told him about it. He thought it would be a dangerous job for me working those hours because someone could attack me, or worse, rape me.

I expected to get a phone call from the truck stop, but I never got one. I gave them a few more days, but nothing happened until I called them. The lady I talked to didn't have any idea about the job ad. I called the company's main office but I couldn't get a hold of someone. I didn't bother to check with them anymore. Maybe that cleaning job was not for me.

I was not scared to do any work. Filipinos were known for that. A couple we talked to at a truck stop in Minnesota who owned a business said they had a lot of Filipino employees, and they liked them because they were all hardworking people. I hoped someone would like me too because I could work as hard as my fellow Filipinos who worked for the couple in Minnesota.

The Receptionist

Marla told me about a company who was always hiring and was only a half an hour drive from Morse Bluff. She said, "I applied there once, but turned it down because the offer was low, and at that time the minimum wage was $6.55, but you should try it now," Marla suggested, "because there's another Filipina who works there too."

I went to the place a few days later, on a Tuesday afternoon; there was no security guard standing inside or outside the front building. That was one thing I noticed; security guards were not like a plague like in the Philippines where every bank, shopping store, drug store, school, hotel, and restaurant, like McDonald's, had at least one security guard. If they were not around, robberies happened.

Once I got into the building, I saw a man sitting in the reception area through a glass door. I told him I was here to apply, and I handed him my one-page résumé that I'd printed at home. He asked me to write my name on the sign-in sheet that was in front of me on the reception counter. He put my résumé on the clipboard and covered it with another form—their company's application form—and told me I could fill it out in the waiting area, then give it back to him once I was done. "Okay, I'll do that," I said.

I read the front and the back of the form and started filling it out. I had to write my social security number on the application form and sign the authorization for a background and a credit check. There was also a question on the form asking if I had any plans of going somewhere in the next six months. I marked an X for "NO," even though I would need time off because I would be delivering our first child five months from then.

I was sure there was a law protecting pregnant women like me if they were applying for a job, but I wasn't going to say anything about my pregnancy unless they asked me. *I'll just tell them after I get hired, if they hire me,* I thought. At the very bottom of the back page of the form the Title VII of the Civil Rights Act of 1964 was written. It said it prohibited employment discrimination based on race, color, religion, sex and national origin.

In the Philippines, I'd never read a law written like that on the application form. Maybe there was, but I'd never paid any attention to it because job discrimination in the Philippines manifested itself. I saw it everywhere—on the classified ads, hiring signs, banners, or posters. Yet, no employers got sued for it. For example, when a shoe store was looking for a saleslady, the listing said:

Wanted:
Female
18-28 years old
5'2" (at least) height
Pleasing personality

Usually, the "pleasing personality" requirement was literal—a beautiful physical appearance. My friend in the Philippines had a two-year secretarial course degree in college, but couldn't find any office job because she was less than five feet tall.

The Title VII also reminded me of the lady truck driver I'd seen at the rest area in Idaho one time. I told Tim, "You won't see a woman driving a truck in the Philippines. It would be odd." But in America, there were no discriminatory requirements, like the height, gender, and the pleasing personality requirement. Also, I didn't need to put a picture on my résumé, which was a common practice in the Philippines.

I checked my application form once again to make sure I didn't miss anything. I gave it back to the man at the reception area. He told me to have a seat again in the waiting area for a short interview. A few minutes later, he came to the waiting area, holding a clipboard, and introduced himself. "My name is Matt," he said, "and I'll be doing the initial interview."

"So, you're from the Philippines?" Matt started.

"Yes," I answered while smiling at him, trying not to look nervous. Matt asked about my call center experiences and a few things about the Philippines; that made me feel comfortable talking with him. The interview lasted ten minutes, and Matt said I could take the tests—written and typing.

Matt asked me to follow him and he told me to sit at the small desk across from the reception area with a white, old desktop computer. He gave me a booklet for my written test, which was an alphabetical order, math, problem-solving, critical and analytical thinking test. "Write the time here when you start and the time when you finish," Matt instructed while turning the pages of the booklet.

After I got done with the written test, Matt came up to me again and explained how the typing test worked. He gave me a paper with the type-written paragraph on it and said, "You have to type it as fast as you can, but don't use a backspace if you make a mistake." Matt set the timer he was holding and told me I had five minutes to do it. I made a few mistakes, I knew it, and I was not sure if I passed this test or not. Matt told me he would forward my application to one of the managers for a review, and they would call me in a week or two if they were interested.

I got a call from Matt a week later, and he asked me if I could come back for a second interview. I was excited knowing that I had a chance to get this job. We set up an interview to meet with a manager.

I met Laura, the manager, at the lobby, and she told me to follow her. Once we sat down in the breakroom, I asked what the business was all about. She said it was a collection agency and their job was to sue people. "I could tell you hurried finishing one test," Laura continued. I knew she was talking about the alphabetical order test because I made a few mistakes at the last part, and she was right, I hurried at that part.

Laura talked about the responsibilities of a receptionist, like answering phone calls, filing, photocopying, etc., and she offered me a starting pay of $7.50 per hour. I had no clue if that offer was high or low because I still didn't know the value of a nickel, a dime, a dollar, ten dollars, or twenty dollars in America. All I knew was $7.50 an hour was a big amount if I converted it to Philippine peso, which was at least forty-five pesos for every dollar, and even if I sent $300 every month to my family, I could still put away some money.

I thought the offer was okay, and I was sure it would increase over time. I told Laura I accepted the job and I asked her when should I start. "Let's start on Monday," she answered. Then we shook hands, and she walked me out the lobby.

I finished the interview without telling Laura that I was five months pregnant. There was no way she would've noticed it because of the thick brown coat I was wearing. I called Tim right away when I got into my car after my interview, and he was excited for me. Tim took me to the mall in Omaha once he got back from trucking to buy my outfit for my new job. I told Tim, "They're all expensive," but he reminded me that it was my first job, and I should have at least one new outfit.

I found beige slacks and a pink, collared, long-sleeve shirt for sixty dollars; I was sure that was expensive. I didn't want to spend another sixty dollars to buy one more set of clothes, so I asked Tim if he could take me to the Goodwill store. "I might find cheaper nice clothes there." I said.

Tim said, "I know a lot of people who don't like to step inside that store, and here you are wanting to go there to buy office clothes."

I told him it didn't bother me at all. That day, we came home with bags of Goodwill clothes and slacks that I would be using next week for my new job. I didn't have to buy a pair of shoes because I could use the ones that we bought at the mall in Lincoln.

On my first day at work, Laura showed me how to clock in at the computer. Then she asked me to sit at one vacant desk in her department. She gave me a W-4 form to fill out for my taxes and the company's manuals and policies to read. On the manual, there was a part about confidentiality, where we had to keep the privacy of every debtor's file.

I was on a ninety-day probationary period where I could not be late or miss a day until I finished my probation, or else it would be extended. I would get benefits, like vacation and sick days leave, 401k program, health and dental insurance, short-term or long-term disability program, and free life insurance after my ninety-day probation.

After I got done filling out the W-4 form and reading the manuals, Laura asked me to file some papers in the drawers in the reception area. Then she sent me home an hour later and told me, "See you tomorrow!"

My work schedule was from 8 a.m. until 5:15 p.m., Monday through Friday. I was happy we didn't have to work on weekends unlike other businesses that were open on weekends, holidays, or open the entire year, like one store downtown with the banner that says they're **"OPEN 365 DAYS!"**

As a receptionist, I had to stay until 5:15 p.m. to close down the reception area and lock the front door. They told me I could clock out at 5:08 because the computer would round off my time to 5:15 pm.

Matt and Laura were training me alternately. They taught me the basics—clocking in and out, printing out job tickets every morning, and answering calls. I also had to write down the time every time a coworker went out of the building so that I knew what to tell someone who was looking for them.

Some co-workers came to talk to me, said hi, and introduced themselves. Just like Matt and Laura, I was having a hard time understanding the words my coworkers said. There were times I just answered yes without really understanding them. But Matt talked slowly, and even when I missed what he said, I just nodded and wrote down what he said on a yellow pad paper.

I was so happy to meet a fellow Filipina co-worker that'd been working there for more than a year. I felt much better knowing I had someone I could talk to in our native Filipino language. That was how it usually worked for a lot of immigrants. By meeting her, I felt I found a new family in a foreign country.

I felt awkward calling my coworkers—the managers, the attorneys, and the company owner—by their first names because that was something I was not used to. In the Philippines, we called our bosses "Ma'am" or "Sir," "Attorney" to lawyers, and "Doctor" to doctors, whenever and wherever we were. We used these addresses as a sign of respect—and subordination.

When I used to work at the call center in the Philippines, some American callers would get mad at me for calling them Sir or Ma'am. I wasn't sure if that made them feel insulted or what, because if I called my boss in the Philippines just by their first name, I would sound disrespectful.

We also called our older brothers or sisters by a special address before their first name, just like the Chinese people do. On the contrary, Americans didn't do the same. They called their older brother or sisters, in-laws, and sometimes aunts or uncles just by their first names. This was part of the American culture I found awkward.

I had trouble understanding some callers on the phone. Answering calls was not hard, just understanding them was the challenge for me. I had to ask one caller if she could spell her three-syllable German last name for me. Most of the time, I received calls from debtors, and all I had to do was tell them to call a different number. There was one debtor who got mad and asked why I couldn't help her.

I also received calls from employers about garnishment; I had to ask Matt what that meant. "It's a court order where the employers take out a certain amount of money from debtor's wages or salary," he explained. Matt also showed me how to print out job tickets, how to use the photocopier, and what to do with the papers I got from some coworkers.

My training only lasted a week. It was a short training, and everything seemed overwhelming.

We got an hour lunch break, and I ate in the break room with a few coworkers. One day, I brought steamed rice and adobo, and that made my coworkers ask me, "What is that?" My lunch was completely different from what they were having—a chef salad, a pizza, or a sandwich, and a yogurt.

Matt and I practiced taking calls. He would call me from a vacant desk and he would pretend to be a debtor, an employer, or someone who had a question. That helped because it made me feel comfortable and confident answering call after call. My day at the office would start with printing out job tickets. Then I would answer calls, and sort and file papers. There were days when a lot of papers needed to be filed, and I had to wait another day to finish them.

When I was filing, it was hard not to look at the papers. I wondered what kind of debts some Americans were trying to run away from. Some debtors owed for medical bills, dental bills, surgeries, rent, electricity, garbage disposal bills, flowers, animal clinic bills, utilities, daycare, telephone bills, returned or bad checks, etc. If I got caught up on filing and I had nothing else to do, I would wipe the phone, clean my desk, or get the pay stub envelopes ready.

There was a UPS guy who picked up a package every afternoon, and he started giving me a hard time. But when he was off, another UPS guy picked up the package, and he asked me if I was from the Philippines. I said yes. He said, "I was stationed in the Philippines in late eighties at the Clark Air Base."

"How'd you get over here?" he asked.

I told him I married an American. He just nodded, but I could tell he wanted to ask me more questions, like if I married someone from the military, which I got asked a lot. When I went to the grocery store one day, a stranger, maybe in his sixties, stopped me in the aisle and asked where I came from. I told him, "I'm from the Philippines." He said he had a friend, also from the Navy, who married an Asian, a Laotian woman, and it worried him because more and more Americans married other nationalities.

"Forty years from now," he said, "Americans like me will be the minority."

I didn't know how to respond to that Navy veteran, but he seemed nice. I didn't want to tell the UPS guy how Tim and I met. He didn't ask further, and when he came back again, we just quickly said hi to each other.

Another part of my job was to help job applicants when they came in and wanted to fill out an application, just like Matt helped me when I applied. I gave them tests if they passed the initial interview and checked each test. It was interesting to read some applicants' forms. Some of them were fired, couldn't keep a job longer than a year, or hadn't worked for years.

It was also surprising to see some applicants who showed up with a newborn baby; one had two young children with her, while one came in with a cute poodle. One applicant came in with her boyfriend. She was young; she had probably just graduated from high school. The manager asked the applicant's boyfriend if he could leave for a little bit so they could do the interview, but he came back a little early and decided to sit and hold his girlfriend's hand.

In the Philippines, you couldn't show up for a job interview with a baby, a cute poodle, or a boyfriend. We couldn't wear whatever clothes we chose; unless it was in the proper dress code. During my job hunting in Manila, the security guards at one company didn't let me get in the building because I was wearing a high-heeled sandal. "No open shoes allowed," the guard said. So, I couldn't imagine what they would've told me if I'd shown up with a puppy.

Those applicants didn't make the testing, and they were told we would call them once the managers were done reviewing their applications. They called a few times to find out if they got the job. I just told them what I'd been instructed to say, even though I'd already filed their application form in the drawer with "NO" written on top of it. I also hoped some of the applicants would know that the job was for a collection agency, and if they owed bills, their accounts got turned over here, which meant stepping into the building was a waste of time for them.

There was another applicant who came in one afternoon and asked me in English if I was a Filipina because she was. I answered in Filipino, "Yes, I am a Filipina." Then both of us started talking in Filipino.

She said, "I'm a singer and part of the Filipino eighties band. My name is Tillie, Tillie Moreno."

Her name didn't ring a bell to me or her band name, and I felt embarrassed. When I got home that day, I researched her name on Google and found out one of her Filipino songs was my favorite. I didn't know she was the original singer of that song because it was revived by a few Filipino artists many times. *It's a small world,* I told myself, but I was glad I met her at the collection agency in a foreign land.

I had to change the bulletin that hung on the wall in the lobby every first of the month. I put the date of each employee's birthday and work anniversary for that month, and they would get a vase of flowers. Some employees had been working there for so long. A couple of them had been there for over twenty years. One manager told me that was her first job when she got out of college. That had me thinking, *Maybe this is a good company to stay with for a long time.*

Tim's friends asked me how I liked my job. I told them, "It's okay; my coworkers are nice."

One friend told me, "Don't be surprised if you see my name on there because of the hospital bill I had when our daughter was born a year ago."

I told her, "You're still lucky because the collection agency goes after you. In the Philippines, collection agencies don't do much business like they do here. A lot of hospitals there won't let you out of the building until your bill is all paid off." It also happens when a mother just leaves the newborn baby at the hospital. But the worst story I've ever heard is when a hospital refused to release the dead patient's body to the family because there's still a balance owed. I don't know why these deplorable practices are tolerated in my home country despite the number of laws that prohibit hospitals of doing it.

Laura was teaching me how to update the company phone list using Microsoft Excel. "We have to do it quarterly," she said. Laura was holding a thick manual procedure for us to follow. "After this training, you'll do the next phone list update by yourself," she said while pulling up another chair.

She sat beside me in the reception area, in front of the computer. She told me we had to copy one file to another window, and I was using the keyboard to do it, but she took the cursor and showed me how to do it. She probably thought I didn't know what I was doing, but I was comfortable using the keyboard—the shortcut keys—because it was easier. It took a while before we finished it, but I promised her I could do it by myself next time.

A caller named Tyler asked to talk to a supervisor, but before I transferred his call, he asked, "If you don't mind me asking where do you come from?"

I told him, "I'm from the Philippines."

"That's what I thought," he said. Tyler worked for a telephone company, and he went to the Philippines a few years ago to be a call center trainer. He said, "The moment I heard your voice, I could tell you were from the Philippines because of your accent."

I didn't know if I would ever lose this accent, even though Tim's friends and my coworkers said I spoke good English and they hardly noticed my accent. I knew it would take time until I acquired that American accent because the way Americans pronounced their words was different from how we spoke English in the Philippines.

There were times when Matt or Laura would ask me to repeat myself because I mispronounced a few words, like one morning when I transferred a call to Laura, she corrected the way I said the word sergeant. I pronounced the word as "SER-jent" instead of "SAR-jent." Even pronouncing names was a challenge for me. I said "Suzanne" instead of "Susan" and I didn't know where to put the diction when pronouncing Daniel or Danielle.

Even a simple word or preposition was confusing sometimes. Matt corrected me when I told a caller that Laura was "on court."

"You should've said Laura was AT court, not ON court," Matt explained.

That day, I learned the difference between the two. It was embarrassing, but I was thankful Matt didn't laugh at me or my mistake, instead he taught me the right way. I looked up prepositions on the computer so that I could learn the proper way of using them. We started studying those in our English class in elementary in the Philippines, but obviously, I didn't pay much attention.

There were still a few words that I had no idea if I was using them wrong. One day, I told a coworker she was a junkie for eating a lot of candy. My coworker gave me the oddest look on earth. I asked Tim, "What's wrong with what I said to my coworker?"

"Junkie is another term for a drug addict," Tim said.

I told him, "I didn't mean it that way because candies are junk food, and that's why I called my coworker a junkie."

That happened whenever I would say words or phrases like I used to in the Philippines, like when we visited Tim's friends one weekend, and I told his funny friend that she had a big butt after I whacked her behind. Tim's friend was startled, but she made this big laugh afterwards. Once we got inside the car, Tim asked me why I did that.

"Did what?" I asked.

"What you just did to my friend. Spanking her butt and tell her she has a big butt," Tim answered.

"Is it bad?" I asked.

"Yes, that's bad to tell someone she has a big butt" Tim said.

"But she's laughing," I defended. Tim just shook his head and told me it was rude.

I hoped my coworker whom I called a junkie and Tim's friend understood that there was a language barrier between us. There were a lot of words that I got confused on and had a hard time understanding.

Tim had a friend who liked to swear, and he told me to excuse his French, which made me more confused because I didn't know that was how they spoke French in America, using the f word and the word shit. I grew up in a home where bad words were forbidden. But I didn't know junkie and saying someone had a big butt (and spanking it) were also rude words to say.

∽

Tillie, my fellow Filipina friend, got hired the following month; we ate lunch in the breakroom upstairs together with our other Filipina coworker. A couple of our American coworkers went there too, but not too often. The three of us shared our food, which usually consisted of rice and a

Filipino dish like pork or beef stew, adobo, egg rolls, or fish.

During lunch one day, we warmed up the smoked fish I brought in the microwave. But it was a huge mistake. We closed the door, but still it smelled. A fuming manager came in with an odor spray in her hand. She started squirting the lunch room while complaining and told us we were not allowed to bring that kind of food again. I overheard another coworker's comment that it made her almost puke.

I knew we were at fault for heating that smelly smoked fish in the microwave. I took responsibility for that incident, and we never did it again. But I just hoped they didn't think all our food—the Filipino or Asian food—was smelly.

When my Filipina coworker brought in ice cream that she made from Durian, a fruit from her province in the Philippines, we asked Matt to try some, but he almost vomited after tasting it. I wasn't offended. Honestly, he made me laugh because at least he tried.

He reminded me of my American friend who tried to eat a cassava cake I made, but she outspokenly said, "It just ruined my meal." The dessert was made from grated cassava root crops, coconut milk, eggs, condensed milk, and cheese. I was not expecting every American to like Filipino food because there was no way they would like all our different stews or eat just a plain white rice. And I didn't think many of them would dare to eat dried fish, smoked fish, or anchovies. Same with Americans, they couldn't expect every Filipino to eat potatoes every day or make them eat steak, even though it was good, because that was something we were not used to.

Marie

I still hadn't told Laura about my pregnancy a month later when I needed to see a specialist in Omaha. My doctor said I had a high-risk pregnancy because I was so small and carrying a breached baby. It was past five o'clock in the evening, and only the two of us were left in the building. I took that opportunity to tell her. Laura didn't look surprised at all. I knew she already knew it.

The following morning, my coworkers came up to me and all congratulated me. One manager said she didn't know I was pregnant, even though I was six months along. "I'm happy for you," she said. My doctor visits became frequent, and I knew my ninety-day probation period would be extended.

The last trimester of my pregnancy became interesting. I felt the heartburn that people had told me about, the tired feeling all the time, but I was lucky enough to have never had morning sickness. I had to ask Matt or Laura to watch the phone for me because of my frequent restroom use.

A couple weeks before my maternity leave started, Laura came up to me and gave me a blank short-sized bond paper and told me to write down what things I still needed for my baby. "We're having a baby shower for you," she said. I was surprised and I wanted to cry in that moment. I'd only been working there for a few months, yet they were doing that for me. In the Philippines, a baby shower was a luxury. It was only for families with money.

Tim's friend asked me, "Do you want the second-hand clothes that my daughter has outgrown?" I said I did. She gave me a lot of baby clothes, a dozen pair of shoes, and other baby equipment, like a bassinet. I remembered that my mother was a midwife and delivered babies for poor couples who had nothing. My mother provided them with baby clothes and formula because they didn't have any money to buy them. *And here I am; I don't have to worry about that,* I thought.

I wrote down stroller, diapers, baby clothes, and receiving blankets and I gave the paper back to Laura. I told our neighbor Erma about the baby shower that my coworkers were having for me, and I told her baby showers were only for rich people in the Philippines. "We just pretend rich here, Gladys," Erma quipped.

The day before my maternity leave began, I had my baby shower where I got everything I listed on the paper. I got a one hundred-dollar store gift card to buy diapers. Laura and another coworker helped me to load the gifts in my car.

My sister-in-law and our friend also gave me a baby shower where I got more diapers, clothes, a sleep mask, and a few more receiving blankets.

My hospital room was nice, very clean, and I didn't have to share the bed with another mother who also delivered a baby, like my friend experienced when she delivered her baby at the public hospital in Manila. My room had a small flat screen TV, a nice, adjustable bed, and I could call the nurse anytime if I needed something. I knew I would remember those little things on my motherhood journey.

We had a baby girl and we named her after my late mother-in-law and also all my sisters, who had Marie in their first or second names. Marie was a healthy and, as my doctor expected, tiny baby; she had to wear preemie size clothes and diapers. A lot of our friends expected that Marie would get all my features, but she came out with lighter skin than mine, rosy cheeks just like an apple, and brown eyes.

"She got your nose, though," my aunt commented on Facebook after I posted a couple pictures. Tim's relatives and our friends, including my two Filipina coworkers, came to visit at the hospital where I got cards, fruits, flowers, and a few more clothes for Marie. Laura came to visit and held Marie for a little while.

The nurse brought Marie to me so that I could breastfeed her. Motherhood was different, full of joy, yet overwhelming. I'd never held a baby that little before, but it seemed like I'd known what to do for so long. People said that came naturally to new mothers like me. I held Marie all the time, and all I did was stare at her, trying to memorize her features. I was too embarrassed to ask the nurse if I could put mittens on Marie's hands, like we do to the babies in the Philippines. Instead, I asked a few questions I was sure other first time mothers asked, like, "Why I don't see tears when she cries?"

A day before we went home, the nurse showed me how to give Marie a bath. The nurse made it look easy, but I was terrified of doing it by myself, yet I couldn't wait to go home with her.

It was gloomy outside when we took Marie home. We waited a day before we went to Dale's and Marge's house. They were both happy and excited to see Marie for the first time. Marie woke up once during our entire visit, and we told Dale and Marge they would be the grandparents, and they were happy about that.

Tim took a couple weeks off to help me around the house, take us to a doctor appointment, and run errands for me. He helped me a lot when I couldn't do much except hold Marie all day.

A few weeks before I gave birth, my friends and coworkers told me to sleep as much as I could before my little one came because I'd be lucky to get three straight hours. And they were right. But Tim was a great help every night when Marie woke up and cried. He picked up Marie, then both of them would head out of the bedroom and sit in the rocking chair in our living room, and Tim would sing a lullaby until Marie fell asleep.

She would wake up and cry again half an hour later. Then it was my turn to pick her up. I appreciated all the help that Tim gave me. The first day I arrived in America, I was worried about living with Tim in case he had any bad behavior or a temper, but he was always kind to me, and I could tell he would be a great father to our daughter. I never saw him get impatient with Marie when she cried non-stop, and he let me sleep unless I had to feed Marie.

Before our wedding, the videographer asked for our pictures to use in our wedding video. Tim brought an album of pictures from when he was a newborn baby until present, but we couldn't find my baby pictures. My mother was not into that. I just loved taking pictures of Marie so that I could keep them, and so that she could have something to look at when she grows up. I knew she could use them someday for an important event in her life, and it would be interesting to see how Marie's face would change—if she still really has my nose when she grows up. We would see that change by keeping the photos, and I couldn't wait to see more in the coming years.

Each night waking up with Marie seemed like it took forever. But two weeks went fast, and Tim was going back to work, which meant I'd be home alone with Marie, who slept during the day and, like an owl, woke at night. She cried because she was hungry, needed a diaper change, or just wanted to be held. Sleeping for two hours straight at night was like winning the lottery. There were times I was too tired to get up, but Marie wouldn't stop crying unless I picked her up, and I didn't get back to sleep until it was almost dawn.

Tim called me a few times a day and asked how I was doing or if Marie was being a good baby or not. I was lucky to fold the laundry or wash the dishes if I could just put Marie in the bassinet without her crying her lungs out. Those couple of days, Marie had been crying like she was in pain, and it worried me. The pediatrician said Marie had colic, and she gave Marie a medication and a certain formula that would help her, and it did.

I decided to stop by at the collection agency so that my coworkers could see Marie. They were happy to see us, and a few of them held Marie. One coworker took off Marie's socks to see her toes. "I have a thing with newborn baby's toes because they're so cute," she said. I'm glad Marie wasn't fussy or crabby that day. All she did was sleep like no one could bother her.

I only had a few days left before I'd be going back to work. Just thinking about that, my days felt heavy, and I was hoping I could stop the clock from turning so that I could spend more time with Marie at home. We visited a couple relatives, and for the first time I met my fellow Filipinas when we went to Marla's son's birthday party. It was nice to meet all of them, and we talked like we've known each other for so long.

A lot of them were from different parts of the Philippines, and they spoke different dialects other than mine. We all spoke Filipino instead. Most of them married Americans and had been living in the U.S. for years. Some of them were in the U.S. on working visas while a couple of them were just like me, new immigrants. I didn't know why, but I was so happy to meet them, and I was comfortable being around them. "I think that is usually how it works when you are in a foreign land meeting your fellow countrymen. Instantly, you become friends and like a family." I told Tim.

There were a lot of questions and funny stories we started sharing. One Filipina said that she'd just gotten fired from her job because she touched her coworker's chest when that coworker told her she didn't wear a bra. Another Filipina said she got reprimanded when she said the word "nigger" to a coworker. These were the things that some Filipino immigrants didn't know that were offensive to do or say—things the people from CFO (Commission of Filipino Overseas) in Manila didn't tell us during our pre-departure seminar.

I also met another Filipina who'd been living in the U.S. since the early nineties. She was also married to an American, and they had two children. They used to live in Hawaii.

I asked her, "How was the first few years of living here back then?"

"It wasn't easy," she answered. "The first time I went to church or at the shopping store, or wherever I went, people stared at me like there was something wrong with my shirt or my face."

She asked her husband, "Why is that?"

Her husband said, "Because a lot of them haven't seen someone like you, someone of different race or color."

"Don't they watch TV and see other people like me?" she asked.

It was also hard for their two young boys because some kids made fun of them. At one time, their boys were chanting "Japanese, Chinese, Filipino!" They would use their index fingers to make slant-eyed gestures. "Japanese, Chinese, Filipino!" Then they did the slant-eyed gesture again.

She asked them, "Where did you learn that?"

The boys told her from the kids at school.

The first time I arrived in my new home town, I asked Tim, "How come I don't see a lot of African-American people or other nationalities like Asians?" I'd seen a few in Omaha when he picked me up at the airport, but when we got out of the city, I didn't see much of them in Fremont and most especially in Morse Bluff, a town with a population of 128.

Tim said, "I have an older sister who's married to a Pakistani, and they have children, but they moved the family from Lincoln to California because some kids were making fun of my nieces and nephew who all have dark complexions and dark hair."

"They moved because Nebraska was not ready for this kind of diversity," his sister said. That was in the nineties. Somehow, I'm thankful I arrived in this country, in this state, in the era where people were more understanding and open-minded to another culture, and people didn't stare at me at the church or any public places because they'd never seen someone like me before. It happened a few times at the restaurant or at the grocery store where some Americans—a man or a woman—took a glimpse of me, and they turned their head the other way when I caught them looking at me. They didn't look in an offensive way; I think they were just curious.

⌒

We just stayed home a few days before my maternity leave was over. I held Marie a lot or took her outside and tried to talk to her like she would understand me. I wanted her to know me well—my voice, my face—before I left her to my friend Marla, who offered to watch Marie while I was at work. I would just pay her every week.

I was dragging my feet the morning I had to go back to work. I had already packed the pink diaper bag the night before with Marie's clothes, blanket, bottles, formula, ibuprofen, diapers, and baby wipes all in it. Both of us woke up before 6 a.m., and I could tell we were both not ready for this.

I didn't know why it was hard for me to leave Marie with Marla, even though I knew she would be okay. I was happy and felt comfortable leaving Marie with her, but I just hoped Marie wouldn't cry that much because Marla had a one-year-old boy, and I was sure watching them at the same time wouldn't be easy. Marla told me I could come over and eat lunch with her so that I could spend time with Marie. I told her I would do that.

My coworkers were excited to see me come back. They asked how Marie was, if I was sleeping, and everything. I didn't know being gone for a month would be so different to where I felt like I had to turn the switch in my head to remember a few things, like printing job tickets, the password on the computer, what button to push to transfer a call. It felt like everything was new to me again, just like the first day Matt was training me. Maybe it was because I had nothing on my mind all day except thinking about Marie.

"Marie only cried when she got hungry," Marla said once I got to her house during my lunch break. I was holding Marie with my one arm while I was eating, and Marla was talking to me. That afternoon when I picked up Marie, Marla gave me a sheet of paper showing how many ounces of the bottles Marie had, the number of diaper changes she did, and things like that. The following day when I dropped off Marie at Marla's house, she told me, "I just got a job, and I can't watch Marie anymore." She recommended a daycare center where I could take Marie. "This is also where I will take my son," she said.

I called the daycare, and they said they had an available spot for Marie, and it was one hundred dollars a week. "You can come over to check out the place," the daycare owner said. Marie and I went to the daycare center the following day, and they gave me a tour of the building. I met Phyllis, a daycare lady who'd been working there for ten years. She was in charge of taking care of the infant room, which had three cribs, one rocking chair, a changing table, and a small refrigerator. Phyllis seemed nice, and I felt comfortable leaving Marie with her.

The first day of dropping off Marie at the daycare was hard. It was harder than when I dropped her off at Marla's house. We arrived early so that I could talk to Phyllis who was sitting on a wooden rocking chair and feeding another baby with a bottle of milk. Phyllis and I talked for a little bit, and she told me I could come here on my lunch break if I wanted to. I said, "I will do that."

Marie was still sleeping in the car seat when I was about to leave, but I was almost crying while heading out the door. I knew Phyllis would take good care of her, and Marie would be fine, but I just couldn't wait for my lunch break so I could hold her. How I wished I could get over that feeling as soon as possible. It was obvious that I was a first-time mother, struggling to leave my child at the daycare.

I remembered when I talked to my mother a few days before I went back to work, and she told me to be brave when dropping off Marie to a babysitter. I tried to be brave every day. I saw some parents leaving their two or three kids at the daycare center, and it seemed those kids were used to being left there. That was something I would have to get used to.

A coworker told me, "It's true that it's hard to do it the first time and harder when your child starts crying and chasing you out the door, but I promise you, they won't remember it." I knew I wasn't at that point yet where Marie was crying and chasing me out the door, and maybe it was true that Marie wouldn't remember it, but one thing was for sure, I was the one who would remember that moment forever.

The following days, things got better every time I dropped off Marie at the daycare. I spent a few lunch breaks at the daycare until I told Phyllis I wouldn't do that anymore because I was very comfortable, and Marie seemed okay. There were mornings I stayed a little longer and talked to Phyllis. She gave me advice about how Marie could sleep through the night, and we talked about other motherly things. I also asked Phyllis about the other baby girl that she was holding.

I noticed since the first day I took Marie to daycare that the baby girl was always there before us, and she was still there when I picked up Marie in the afternoon. "Her mother drops her off at six o'clock in the morning because she has to drive to work," Phyllis said. I felt bad for this girl. That was the reason I couldn't wait to clock out from work every afternoon so that I could pick up Marie as soon as possible because I missed her so dearly.

That left me wondering if that was how they did it in America—that daycare was part of most young children's lives while growing up. In the Philippines, daycare centers were not a big business. I'd never seen a daycare center while I was still living there, and if there were some operating, then they were only for rich people who could afford to shell out that kind of money. A lot of kids spent more time at daycare than at home with working parents. I couldn't wait to pick up Marie every afternoon, and the two of us either went to the grocery store or drove straight home. I played with her in the playpen for a little bit before I started cooking for supper. I also held Marie as much as possible because I always felt guilty for not seeing her all day while I was at work.

⤲

A few weeks into taking Marie to daycare, Martha, the daycare owner, called and asked about the big bruise on Marie's bottom when I had just gotten to my work place when. "Phyllis noticed it while she was changing Marie's diaper," Martha said, sounding worried. I told Martha that Marie was a breached baby and that big bruise was caused by sitting on my uterus for so long. The doctor said it would fade away over time.

I could hear a relief in Martha's voice. They probably thought something happened to Marie, like we dropped or abused her. I was thankful Martha called me first, not the Child Protection Services, who could've come into my work to talk to me or, worse, taken Marie away from us. I felt bad for not telling Phyllis about Marie's bruise the first day, but I didn't know it would worry the daycare staff like that.

⌒

Marie was only two months old and already recognized me. She was looking straight at me when I was picking her up from daycare, even while she was being held by daycare staff. Marie would start crying after she saw me. There were times I wished I was a stay-at-home mother, but having a child in America was expensive. That was why Tim kept driving trucks, even though he didn't like doing it since we had Marie. "But we have bills to pay," Tim always said.

I noticed a fifty-cent increase on my first pay check after I got back from maternity leave. I was now making eight dollars per hour. I thanked Laura for working the raise out while I was on leave. For some people, this increase would not be much, but I couldn't complain because it was better than nothing. That small increase would somehow help with paying our bills.

⌒

At three months old, Marie was having her baptism at St. George Catholic Church. The priest visited us at home one night and had both of us sign paperwork. Then he told us about the Holy Sacrament of Baptism. Tim's relatives, our friends, and my Filipino friends were coming to the Baptism.

Marie would have two godparents—one godmother and one godfather—which was different from in the Philippines, where you could have as many godparents as you wanted. My brother-in-law and my sister Arianne were Marie's godparents, but since my sister was in the Philippines, a Filipina friend stood as a proxy. We served Filipino and American food at the reception and we were happy to welcome Marie as a Catholic baby. We were also happy that this baptism was out of the way because we'd been busy for a few weeks between preparing for it and moving to the house we just bought!

Buying a House

A couple months before Marie's Baptism, we found a foreclosure two-story house in North Bend, just two miles away from Morse Bluff. We didn't have a hard time getting a mortgage loan, but we had a high interest rate on it because of my credit history—I had none. The loan officer advised me that paying mortgage on time would help me build my credit. We bought the house because our mortgage payment would be the same as our rent in Morse Bluff.

The house had four bedrooms—two downstairs and two upstairs—but there was no basement. It had a two-car garage and a big backyard where we could see our neighbor's horses and Marie could play in the summer. The kitchen was bigger than the one we had in Morse Bluff. There was a small laundry room and one bathroom.

That was what Tim promised me the day I arrived in America, to own a house someday. The house was old, and there was a lot of work to do. All the walls needed to be painted, the carpets needed to be replaced, and the whole house needed to be cleaned. I picked the paint colors inside the house while Tim took care of the outside. I picked a cream color for in the kitchen, pink in Marie's bedroom, and white paint in the master bedroom, the two rooms upstairs, and the bathroom.

Tim cleaned the house for hours on his days off and when he got off work. I asked him to have someone cut the big tree in front of the house because it creeped me out when the wind was blowing at night and I was all alone with Marie. The tree was cut a few days later.

We bought a new sectional, oven, and refrigerator, which we got for half-price because it had a "ding" on the side. The bed, mattress, dresser, dining table, washer, and dryer all came with us to our new home. Moving was the hardest part. Tim only found one person to help him move that day, and I felt bad for not helping because I couldn't lift those heavy appliances. I helped pack clothes, plates, and other things and put them in boxes or black garbage bags. We put a few boxes upstairs.

Tim asked me to come with him one weekend afternoon to meet our neighbors, who were both retired, for the first time. They were showing us their big family photo on the wall, telling us who was who. There were a few pictures in black and white that looked classic.

"That was me," Bob said, pointing at the picture of a young man wearing a suit.

"You were handsome, Bob," I complimented.

"Were? And not now?" Bob asked, laughing hard.

"I'm sorry for what I just said, but I didn't mean it that way," I told him. "You're still handsome, even now that you got old."

All of us were laughing, especially Bob.

We had another neighbor who lived by himself, but we hardly saw him there. The guy seemed to be gone all the time, but Tim said he'd already met that neighbor. I hoped I would meet him. We also met our ninety-two-year-old neighbor who lived by herself. I didn't know it was part of the culture in America for retired people to either live by themselves or stay at the nursing homes.

In Daet, it was rare to see people like them living without any company of grandchildren or an adult child. My grandmother never lived alone. We stayed with her since we were young, then my cousin's teenage son stayed with her. That was simply our culture, and seeing that difference only left me in wonder. But one thing I was sure of was that we would enjoy our new house. We were at the end of the town where it was quiet and the small gate between our house and garage gave us more privacy.

⌒

After a few weeks, we started unpacking boxes that we had just put upstairs during the move. It took weeks for us to get everything settled inside the house. Tim asked me, "Where did you put all the photo albums?"

"What photo album?" I asked.

Tim was looking for a photo album that had his Filipina ex-girlfriend's pictures in it, and I knew what he was talking about.

I told him, "I tossed them in the trash can when I was packing up in Morse Bluff. I don't understand why you keep those when there's no reason for it."

"For memories," he said.

﹏

We celebrated our first Halloween in that house by putting a big carved pumpkin and a couple small pumpkins on the glider outside. Marie was wearing a pumpkin hat, a white long-sleeve shirt that had "My First Halloween" written on it, and orange pants. We handed candies to the trick-or-treaters, and one of them was a girl, maybe ten years old, wearing a witch costume with green lipstick. She told me, "We used to live here." Maybe that was why I noticed her looking at our house when I opened the door. We hadn't heard much of anything about the previous owner of this house, except that it went to foreclosure.

﹏

Marie slept in her crib in her own bedroom, where she had a lot of room to crawl around—or play in the coming months. I was happy we got this house, and there was a nice feeling owning it, but there were a few weird incidents that happened, like when I was preparing our dinner one night and someone knocked on the door. I could see a man through the pink blinds on our glass window. I opened the door, and a young man, probably as old as me at the time, introduced himself with his memorized script. He looked like he'd just taken some happy pills with the wide smile on his face. He asked if I would be interested in buying their vacuum.

"We have a vacuum," I said.

There was another man with him, standing outside of their car that was parked in front of our house.

He said, "We can show it to you quickly."

The other man ran to their car and came back holding a long box. They insisted on showing it to me. I let them in. They took off their shoes, and we all went to the living room. When they started opening the box, the smiling guy asked, "Where's the electrical outlet to plug it in?"

I stopped them and said no. They both looked at me, wondering.

"My husband is sleeping and you'll wake him up if you run it," I told them.

"Oh!" the guy with the smiling face said. They probably thought no one was with me except Marie, but Tim was sleeping in our bedroom after trucking overnight. I didn't want him to come out without his shirt on, see these guys vacuuming our living room, and ask me, "What the heck is going on?"

I told the guys I was not going to buy their vacuum anyway, and then they left. I checked online about their company and all I read was scam, scam, scam. People made bad reviews on this company who would vacuum your carpet for a few minutes, then make you buy it. "These salespeople get rude and nasty," most reviewers wrote. I was just thankful those two guys didn't say any bad words or insist I buy their vacuum.

Not too long after that there was another salesman who was selling children's books. I told Tim I wasn't interested, but he let him in, and all of us ended up wasting our time sitting at the kitchen table. We didn't buy anything because they were so expensive, and Marie already had tons of children's books.

I told my coworker about these incidents, and she said, "They do that to foreigners like you. They think you're the easy target because these people think you can't say no to them." I said, "But too bad those guys knocked on the wrong door and didn't make me buy their vacuum or children's books."

Other than salespeople, a cop showed up at our door a couple times at night; that made me feel worried and embarrassed. Having a cop standing at my front door was the last visitor I wanted to have. The first time a cop showed up, he was asking for someone who was living in the house. I told him maybe that was the previous owner because we just moved here. The cop seemed like he didn't believe me because he kept looking past me. He apologized and left.

The next time a cop showed up was also at night, and he asked me if I'd ever seen our neighbor—the one I hadn't met yet—walking on his patio just with his underwear on. He told me someone called and complained. I told him no.

⌇

Marie and I spent a lot of time doing the same routine from Monday to Friday. We would wake up at six o'clock in the morning; I would give her a bottle and put her in the crib while I took a shower. A lot of the time, I didn't eat breakfast at home; I just brought food to work or bought a cinnamon roll at the café near the office building.

We were running late one morning because Marie and I had a long night, and I walked out the door wearing one of two different pairs of black shoes. It was a good thing my black slacks hid it, and no one ever noticed at my workplace.

My days at work became easier, and I was trying really hard not to miss a day or be late because I was still on the probationary period. I kept learning a lot of things, meeting new people, and getting different calls, like a call from a single mother who was upset and crying because her bank account was garnished. "I have young children to feed. How could you do that to me?" she asked. I felt her frustration, but I couldn't do anything except listen to her sentiments and tell her to call a different number, even though I was sure they would tell her it was a court order and they couldn't do anything about it.

When I used to work at the call center in Manila, I never had any sympathy for customers who cried over losing their satellite service because of non-payment. Some customers cried because they couldn't watch their favorite show or the weather channel. I knew those people could survive without watching TV, and it was a waste of tears to cry about that. But people like a single mother with young children who was crying on the phone because her bank account was almost empty deserved some sympathy. Other than that kind of call, I still did the same job everyday—printing job tickets, filing, sorting, answering phone calls—until the day was over and I was ready to pick up Marie.

ᔱ

Marie turned five months old, and there she was, already learning how to crawl. It was incredible to see her milestones each day. *It seems just like yesterday when I was holding her for the first time at the hospital as a newborn baby. A few months from then she's crawling. Soon she'll be standing up, then walking, and by that time she'll be a sister.* I thought, sitting in the bathroom with my hands shaking while looking at the pregnancy test I'd just taken. I saw two clear red lines.

I told Tim, who was in the kitchen cleaning up the table while holding Marie. He had a surprised look on his face, and asked me if I was serious.

"I am," I answered while holding up the pregnancy test result.

He told me, "It's your birthday present from me."

I was ashamed to see my doctor again, who asked me at the hospital after giving birth to Marie if I would like to be on a pill or any contraceptive because I might get pregnant right away. "It's happened to some of my patients," he said.

I told him, "No, thanks. I'll be all right and I'll pray hard." But my prayer didn't seem to work out well.

"You're due next summer," my doctor said. Marie would be only thirteen months older than her new sibling.

I told the news to my coworkers after my doctor's appointment, and one manager asked Laura, "Doesn't she know how to use contraceptives so she doesn't get pregnant too soon?" That manager didn't know I was around. I just ignored what she said.

⁓

I was happy to have my first Christmas party with my American coworkers. We had a gift exchange and a potluck. In the Philippines, companies usually provided food, games, prizes and gifts, while other companies rented a nice place to celebrate for a bigger and merrier Christmas party. We also received a thirteenth-month salary and a bonus, but it was different in America.

My coworkers brought a variety of food, snacks, and cookies, but I decided to bring *buko salad,* a shredded fresh coconut with cocktail fruits, and condensed milk. I gave it to Laura that morning, and she put it in the fridge upstairs. But we forgot to bring it over to the other break room where we had our party. I also got a sixty-five-dollar bonus check because we met our collection goal. *Not bad for the amount, at least, we got something for Christmas,* I thought. The company gave us a store gift certificate for a ham or turkey. I chose turkey because this would be the first time I'd prepare it. My coworker said it was easy to prepare, "Just clean it, pat dry with paper towels, put butter all over, then bake it according to the package label instructions."

⌒

Driving to work in winter was not exciting when I had a baby with me. I always bundled Marie with warm clothes and drove slowly. I felt nervous when it was snowing outside, even though the highway was cleared. I wanted to quit my job so I wouldn't have to drive in the snow with Marie in the backseat. I kept the 60-mph speed limit on the highway, but there were mornings I chose to drive slower than that. I didn't want something bad to happen to us, but an accident occurred one morning when we were close to the daycare.

A young gentleman hit my car from behind, and I hit the car in front of me. I was scared when Marie cried that hard. Thank goodness no one got hurt. Marie just got scared. I didn't hit my head or face on the steering wheel, but the strong force from behind made my neck hurt, and Marie got scared. The cop said, "It's a good thing you were all wearing seat belts, and Marie was buckled up good."

But what worried me was the pregnant lady in the car I hit. She said, "I'm almost due, but I'm okay." There was slight damage to the front and the back of my car.

I tried not to miss a day of work so that I could finish my probationary period. No matter how bad the road was, I still had to go to work. If Tim had the day off, I asked him to give me a ride. I didn't want my probationary period to get extended again. I was so happy when I finished my probationary period. I could use the prorated vacation days—two days—for my doctor appointments. I wouldn't go as frequently as I used to when I was pregnant with Marie, but there were times I had to extend my lunch hours because of an appointment.

I talked to some mothers at the daycare, and one mother told me about Title Twenty. I had no idea what it was. That mother said, "It's a childcare subsidy program that I'm getting for my daughter because my income qualifies to the state's poverty guideline." She suggested I apply too because it really helped, but I was hesitant to do so after a coworker told me he couldn't qualify to get help for paying their utilities. "My income exceeds the income limit," he said.

It surprised me because I was sure both of us didn't get paid that much from our company. I was still earning eight dollars an hour; maybe he made a dollar more per hour than me, but he was the breadwinner in his family with one child. It made me wonder about our chances of getting qualified when Tim and I were both working.

Still, I submitted an online application, and a few weeks later, we got a letter from the state saying we got approved for the childcare assistance program where the state would pay Marie's daycare cost—$400 a month. It did really help, but it didn't last long when Tim switched jobs, from being an owner-operator to a company truck driver. We received a letter from the state saying the benefit was ending because our income was more than the poverty limit after they did an income verification. The following months became financially challenging for us. Tim and I tried not to miss work every day so that we could make it month by month.

Olivia

In August 2011, we welcomed our second child, another healthy baby girl, who we named Olivia. She had brown hair and darker skin than Marie, who had just turned one year old a month prior. Olivia had jaundice; her skin and the white of her eyes were yellowish. After we brought her home, the doctor advised me to make sure she got enough sunlight every day, and we made a couple trips back to the hospital for check-ups and a test. It didn't take long for Olivia to get over this condition.

It was hard having two children so close together. But the nurse who took care of me at the hospital said it was okay to have children that close in age. Hers were only ten months apart. She said she got pregnant four weeks after she gave birth to their oldest child. "But they're just like best friends growing up, and you will raise them all at once," she said. Every time she came to my room, we had a conversation, from babies to our personal lives. She asked me how Tim and I met, and I told her our story. "That's crazy," she exclaimed.

I asked how she met her husband, but instead she said she just got divorced from her husband of thirty-five years who cheated on her. "I'm not enough for him," she said while she was checking the IV on my left hand. I didn't know how to react to stories like this except saying "I'm sorry to hear that." I could hear the loneliness in her voice and I didn't ask more. On our last day at the hospital, she told me to enjoy my daughters and for sure they'd keep me busy.

I could tell Marie was jealous every time she saw me holding Olivia. Marie didn't know what to think of her little sister the first day we brought Olivia home. I wondered if it was jealousy or curiosity. There were times Marie would look at me while I was holding Olivia, then pull Olivia's hand, foot, or tap her head.

I thought, *She doesn't really know what she's doing,* or *Maybe she just wants to hold her little sister.* I had her sit on the couch one day after she bit Olivia's toes. I thought it was because she was teething, but she always came to me and wanted me to hold her too. Marie's pediatrician told me to spend time with her whenever I could because at her young age, she would still get jealous. There were times I let Tim hold Olivia while I played with Marie outside, and she really loved it. I felt guilty for always giving her milk in a sippy cup instead of giving her the attention she was asking.

Just like last year, I wasn't excited about going back to work when my maternity leave was over. Our daycare cost for both babies was $183 a week, and I asked myself if it was really worth it to go back to work because the total amount for daycare was more than half of my monthly paycheck. My friend recommended that I consider working at the daycare because some daycares gave discounts for that, but I didn't bother to try. I still went back to work even though I wouldn't make that much money after taking out the daycare expenses and gas money. I talked to my family in the Philippines and told them we wouldn't send money every month because of the expenses we had. They understand, and it was a good thing Arianne had just graduated from college and started looking for a job.

Dropping off the girls for the first time was harder than the first day I dropped off Marie at daycare last year. Marie was chasing me, crying, and calling me like I was leaving her there forever. She wanted me to hold her, and I did. She quit crying, and I told her "I'll go and buy you a toy and I'll be back soon," but that didn't work out when I put her back down. Phyllis told me I could go, and she picked up Marie with her mournful cry. I could still hear Marie's cry while I was heading out the door. I sat inside the car, almost crying, and Tim called wanting to know how everything went.

Green Card

In mid-September 2011, we went back to Immigration Services in Omaha for my two-year conditional permanent residency interview. I passed the interview and I received my ten-year permanent resident card a couple months later. Just looking at the card, I knew why they called it a "green card"—because of its color. Having two daughters, a receptionist job, a nice home, a reliable car to drive, and a green card on hand, I felt my life was full. Three years after that, I could file for U.S. citizenship.

Laura came up to me one morning and told me she was quitting her job. I stopped sorting papers and I looked at her with surprise and sadness. She'd been nice to me since day one, and I wouldn't forget that interview we had at the breakroom. She made me feel comfortable working there. Now that she was leaving, I wanted to quit too, but I couldn't. A few weeks later, we got a new manager, Mary, who took over Laura's job.

⌒

Two years passed and everything was still the same at work—the monotonous morning routine at the reception area, sorting and filing papers, photocopying, asking visitors to sign-in with their names, giving the UPS guy a hard time, assisting job applicants, getting phone calls from debtors, employers, lawyers, marketers, etc., etc. I called in a few times because either Marie or Olivia got sick or I had to leave work early because the daycare staff said one of them was running a temperature. I really wanted to quit when Mary handed me two notices showing the percentage of my tardiness and absences because of that. "It's high," Mary noted.

Tim and I started considering finding different jobs where we wouldn't have to take the girls to daycare or I wouldn't have to drive to work. I won't forget when I almost had an accident after I spun three times on the icy road. It was a good thing Tim was off that day and watched the girls at home. Maybe that was a sign that I had to find another job. I told Tim I would study medical billing online and once I get done with the class, I could work at home. It will take me a year to finish the course, but I would try hard to get it done.

I celebrated my second-year anniversary at the collection agency, and I got a five-day vacation leave. I told Mary I was using the days for our vacation to the Philippines that spring because it'd been almost four years since I had seen my family.

Philippine Vacation

We found cheap tickets for our flight in the first week of May 2013, and we were taking a three-week vacation. My family was excited to see Marie and Olivia for the first time. But going back to the Philippines was expensive, even though we didn't have to pay for Olivia because she was a "lap child." Still, we had to come up with $4000 for our plane tickets, and we were using the tax refund money we'd just gotten to pay for our fare. We were bringing $1500 with us to pay for our hotel, fares, food, souvenirs, and if there was any leftover money, I would give it to Nanay, my sisters, and my mother. Tim worried that the money wouldn't be enough, but I promised him I would try to budget that money.

Frank took us to the Eppley Airport in Omaha for our 6:00 a.m. flight. Even though this was a hassle for Frank, he was willing to pick us up at 3:30 a.m. from our house. I knew this departure time would be hard for the girls, but we had no choice but to take the early flight because it was cheaper. We were so thankful to have Frank as a friend even though we were not neighbors anymore.

The airline lady at Eppley airport kept us for half an hour because every time she scanned my passport, we heard a beep sound. She insisted I needed a visa in Guam. I told her I didn't need a visa because my travel agent told me all I needed was my Philippine passport and my green card. I knew Guam was still part of the United States, and my green card would be okay there. Tim and I were getting worried, hoping we wouldn't miss our flight. Finally, the lady figured it out, and she gave me my boarding pass. She said, "Don't lose it because there's a special instruction written on it."

The girls started crying when the plane was taking off. I asked them to "Say ah!" but it didn't work. They cried for a little bit, but I was thankful they were not screaming like I thought they would. I had Olivia on my lap, and Tim was sitting beside Marie. We still had long hours ahead of us—from Houston to Hawaii to Guam then Manila. It was almost a one-day flight. The girls slept most of the time on the airplane, but carrying them at the airport while finding our plane gate made me want to go back to Nebraska and wait for another year to take this three-week vacation. An airport employee offered to carry Olivia while Tim was carrying Marie. I was thankful that strangers offered help in this big and busy airport in Houston, Texas.

Four years before our trip, I was so happy to see America up from the sky; then there I was, so excited to see the Manila skyline a few thousand feet away. I saw the slow-moving traffic, the buildings, the city lights, and the big Ninoy Aquino International Airport. It felt just like yesterday when I was inside that airport, pulling one black suitcase, nervous yet excited to fly for the first time to go to America and live with Tim.

The plane landed at 8:30 p.m. My sisters, Con, Arianne, and Charlotte, were picking us up, but they were not there yet. I didn't have a phone to call or text them, but I had their phone number written on a piece of paper. We had the airport cart full of our luggage, and Tim let Olivia sit on top of it. Marie was standing beside me and holding my hand. Tim was wondering too why we hadn't seen our sisters at the waiting area across the street. I told him they might be stuck in traffic, but half an hour past, and my sisters were still not there.

The Filipina who had also just arrived let me use her cellphone. I offered to pay her, but she refused. I talked to my oldest sister, Con, and she said, "We just left our place an hour ago." Clearly, they were running late. Their place was only an hour away from the airport, but because of the traffic, I wouldn't have been surprised if they'd shown up three hours later.

"What? There's no way you could be here within two hours because of the traffic," I said to my sister in our dialect, with frustration in my voice.

"Why would they make us wait for hours when they know we have our daughters with us who are now so tired and start getting crabby?" I said to Tim.

That was one thing I really appreciated about living in America; I learned so much about the value of time. Showing up on time to any appointment, whether they were that important or not, showed you had respect for someone else's time, and being on time was a sign of maturity. Tim and I were exhausted too, after not getting any sleep on the airplane because of the girls. We went back and forth to the Duty Free store a few times, not because we were buying chocolates or souvenirs for my family, but to get some cool air. Tim and the girls were getting sweaty and both girls wanted to be held.

At 11:30 p.m., my sisters finally arrived, all smiles; they kept apologizing and blaming each other. My sisters explicitly showed Tim what Filipino time really meant—always late, not half an hour, which is more forgiving, but three hours late. I got over my irritation with my sisters the moment they were coming to us, and they held the girls right away. Olivia cried when Charlotte started kissing her. It was funny to see how they reacted toward their aunts, and all of us were laughing.

Manila was still the same—the heat, congested traffic, and people were everywhere, with the notion that people from America were always loaded with money. I had already told my sisters we didn't have a lot of money to spend on them, but we had Hershey's candy bars and clothes in two suitcases, and they could have them once we got into the hotel. We were only staying in Manila for a couple days, then we'd go to Daet. I couldn't wait to see my family and take the girls to the beach. My sisters were coming with us, and they would be a big help with our daughters while riding the bus, and we rented a motel room where Tim and the girls would feel comfortable.

It took us a while before we could put our things in the motel room when the manager changed our rate; it was doubled. She insisted there was a misunderstanding between her and my mother who made the motel reservation a few weeks prior. I originally reserved for a big room with the kitchen where I could cook during our entire stay for a very affordable price, but we ended up choosing a smaller and cheaper room instead. My family was thinking the only reason the manager changed her mind—and the motel rate—was because she saw Tim, a foreigner with lots of dollars.

The motel room had an air-conditioner, a cold shower, a small TV, and two beds. We got a lot of company every day, and the girls played with their cousins. My mother and Nanay held the girls a lot, and if they could've only squeezed them, they would have. Some of their little cousins touched the girls' hair and asked me if it was real or if I dyed their hair.

Every time we went to restaurants or the mall, people always looked at them. "They look like dolls, living dolls," one saleslady gushed when we were looking for a t-shirt for Tim. The salesladies swarmed our daughters and started speaking English, and they all giggled when they heard Marie speak with her American accent, while another saleslady told me the girls were so cute.

"Are you their nanny?" she asked.

"No, I'm their mother," I told the saleslady, who looked embarrassed and said sorry. We walked out of the store without buying a t-shirt.

Nanay told me to dress up nicely, not too simple like what I was wearing—a t-shirt and a pair of pants.

She said, "You should wear something that people in town will know that you just came from America, married to an American, and have two daughters with brown hair, light skin, and speak English." The only jewelry I wore was my wedding ring that Tim bought me at the jewelry store in Fremont. Nanay wanted me to dress up like other Filipinos who'd come back to the Philippines for a vacation. The ones who show-off.

People in town asked me how my life was in America, what my job was there, why I was still skinny when my sisters who lived in Manila were not, and they asked if I could speak English to them so that they could hear that "American accent."

Tim and I got sick one day, and we thought it was because of the calamari we ate at the restaurant, but we found out it was because of the tap water we drank. I forgot what my Filipina friend in Nebraska told me about drinking tap water there. Our stomachs were not used to the water. "How crazy it is to think that even your stomach is no longer a Filipino for being that sensitive," my mother said to me in our dialect.

Marie enjoyed her time with her cousins. She read a book while sitting in a hammock with her cousins who were trying so hard to speak English with her. Marie got a wound on her knees when she fell on the ground when they were playing tag games, while Olivia acted like the snobbish one who wouldn't go to anyone except to me, Tim, and my grandmother. But we were all having fun, and Tim enjoyed the simple birthday celebration we had for him. I ordered a small hog roast and a cake.

If only we'd had a lot of time, I would've taken my family to different places and visited friends, but we only went to Bagasbas Beach a couple times. Olivia didn't know what to think every time small waves hit her feet. She would cry and run to me to hold her, but Marie was having a blast running and giggling when she felt the water on her feet. I could tell she liked it—the beach, the sand, the shells she found, and her family with her. She looked like she was living in the best world. That was their first time seeing the ocean, and they might've been too young to remember that, but I could tell they were so happy being there.

I also got a chance to visit Ma'am Wava (pronounced as Way-Va), the registrar I worked for when I used to be a student assistant in the state college where I graduated. Ma'am Wava became like a special person to me. She was nice and helped me financially when I was struggling to make it to finish my college education.

We stayed so late at her office to finish manually recording all the grades of the students. Even though she wasn't paid for the overtime hours she put it, still, she gave me money for staying late with her. She would bring extra food for her lunch to share it with me and with two other student assistants. There were times she took us to eat out, all her expense. We talked about a lot of things, about my life, my family, and my goals in life. She gave me a lot of advice, and in that one year of working with her, we became so close. I made her one of our sponsors, and she was the one who made our wedding cake. Before I immigrated to the U.S., she took me to a spa and both of us enjoyed the foot spa.

Ma'am Wava was so happy to see me and Marie. Tim and Olivia stayed at the hotel because the two of them were not feeling well. Ma'am Wava couldn't believe that I visited her. "I thought you already forgot me," she said. I told her there was no way I would do that. She asked me how my life was in America. We talked about a lot of things, and before Marie and I said goodbye to her, we took some pictures together.

We tried everything to make our visit a happy one, but the only problem we had was getting short on money. Tim was right; the $1500 we brought wasn't enough for the three-week vacation. We were expecting money to be deposited to our bank account in Nebraska while in Daet, but when we called our banker, he said it would be delayed a couple more weeks.

I had to make another long-distance call to Mary at work, asking her to give my paycheck to my Filipina coworker so that she could deposit it into our bank account. "She already knows about it. I just sent her a Facebook message," I told Mary. But Mary said I would still need an authorization to do that. "This is my authorization," I told her over the phone, but Mary insisted I still needed an authorization letter. Then the phone got disconnected. Mary probably thought I got mad and hung up, but I ran out of minutes. My Filipina coworker sent me a Facebook message saying Mary gave her my paycheck, and she deposited it into our bank right away.

I hoped we wouldn't wait too long to come back here again; I didn't know if it would be another three or four years of waiting. How I wished our vacation was more than three weeks, but we had to go back to U.S. in a few days.

We stayed in Manila three days before our departure. We were staying at the same hotel where we stayed when we first arrived. My sisters come to visit and spend time with us. They held the girls most of the time—a proof that they would miss them so much.

We had the same route going back to the U.S.— Manila, Guam, Hawaii, Houston, then Omaha, but once we got to Houston, we missed our flight going to Omaha because of the change they made on our itinerary. The plane from Hawaii to Houston got delayed, and they only gave us a thirty-minute layover time which was impossible to make. We waited another four hours, and we called Frank to let him know about the delay. It was a hassle from the beginning to the end of that flight. We just let our daughters run around and play in the waiting area until we started boarding for our flight to Omaha.

Frank was waiting for us at the airport, and we thanked him again, but he told us not to worry about it. The girls and I slept in the car all the way home while Tim, who was sitting next to Frank, talked until we were home. Tim said I was speaking Filipino to them when I woke up from the back seat and Frank asked him what I was talking about.

"I have no idea," Tim told Frank, smiling and shaking his head. I was thankful to be home, and even though we were exhausted, I took a shower and gave the girls a quick bath. We didn't bother to eat anything, and the four of us went to bed right away. I was fighting the same jet lag like when I first got over to the U.S. I was not sure if it would take the same length of time to get over it. Just like before, everything seemed new to me—the air, the quiet surroundings, driving the car, and holding the steering wheel. Even going back to work felt odd.

Quitting

Two months after we got back from the Philippines, Mary was giving me my yearly evaluation. She said I wouldn't get a raise because of my tardiness and a few absences I had. I told her I had to because of my daughters who got sick. Mary asked if I had any relatives or friends who could take care of them if it happened again. I reminded her that my family was in the Philippines. "And if you're talking about Tim's family members, I doubt if they could help me because they also have jobs and have their own families to take care of, and I don't have friends that would watch them when they're sick." I said. She still told me I wouldn't get a raise that year.

Making eight dollars an hour was not enough for someone like me who had two daughters who attended daycare. Tim took a custodian job at the school near where we lived, even though it didn't pay that much. It saved money by not driving to work, and he didn't have to work overnights and weekends too.

A few weeks after that evaluation with Mary, I started looking for another job. Tim and I both decided that was what was good for our daughters. I thought I would become a medical billing specialist, but I didn't finish the entire course. I lost my interest in pursuing it. I decided to find a job somewhere. I put in my application at the recycling place, where I didn't need any experience for the office job, but I never got a response.

I also filled out an application to a company that provided services for developmentally disabled people, but I cancelled my interview after I talked to a Filipina friend who'd already been doing this kind of job. "With your small body frame, there's no way you could last long because a lot of the patients are way heavier and bigger than you. You would have to help them to get up from their wheelchair and assist them walking or going somewhere." my friend said, begging me not to do it.

I looked for another job, this time at the nursing home that was looking for a dishwasher. I turned it down when the lady told me what the working hours were. The schedule wouldn't work for us.

A Filipina friend suggested that I try working at the convenience store in our town, even just for a year or until the girls went to school; then find another job I liked. I dropped by one afternoon at the store, and I talked to a gentleman at the cash register about getting a job there. They had an ad in the paper saying they were looking for a kitchen crew member. The gentleman gave me an application form to fill out, and he said I could take it home with me and return it once I was done. I submitted an online application, but I never heard from them or received any rejection letter. I wanted to work there, hoping I'd get a schedule that would work out for us. I was hoping I could work in the morning while Tim watched our daughters, then I'd watch them in the afternoon while Tim worked until night.

I got the job and the schedule I wanted. I gave my two-week notice to Mary after I accepted the job as a kitchen helper. The gas money, the driving time, and the daycare expenses were things I didn't have to worry anymore by taking this new job. The morning I gave my resignation notice, Matt came up to me and said, "You know I'm not happy about it, but I understand."

I would miss some of my coworkers, especially Matt, whom I'd talked to about a lot of different things, from current events to his dogs. One afternoon when he asked me what my middle name was, I told him, "My mother's maiden name because that's how the law works in the Philippines." Matt told me he would freak out if I said "Faye" because that was his dog's middle name, "Gladys Faye!" I told him Faye was Olivia's middle name.

Somehow, I was thankful I'd worked for the collection agency, where I learned a lot of things.

By answering phone calls, I learned more words like reviver, deposition, and other legal terms. Also, I met people and I knew what it was like to work with Americans, and that was one experience I wouldn't forget.

Kitchen Crew Member

When I found the kitchen job at the store, there were a couple people who made me feel like it was beneath me or a job they wouldn't take for anything. A coworker at the collection agency laughed when I told him about taking the job. I didn't know what was funny about working at the convenience store, but I told him the reasons why I took the job. Tim was working as a school janitor, and I'd be working at the convenience store, making pizza and cheeseburgers. I didn't mind doing this if our daughters would be able to stay home with us all the time; they wouldn't get sick as often, and we wouldn't have to drive that far.

My starting pay was eight dollars an hour, and I'd get a fifty-cent raise right after my ninety-day probationary period; then a twenty-five-cent increase every year. The store manager, Tonya, suggested I start as part-time to see how I liked it. The store was open twenty-four hours, seven days a week.

I'd start working at six o'clock in the morning until noon, four or five days a week. I'd be making pizza and sandwiches, taking pizza orders, and preparing breakfast and lunch food for the warmers.

Tonya also pitched to me the job of making donuts because they were needing another person. She said their donut maker only worked on weekdays, from Sunday until Thursday. It was an overnight shift, from eleven o'clock at night until six or seven o'clock the next morning. "You would get an extra fifty cents an hour if you do it," Tonya said, trying to convince me. I told her I'd think about it.

On my first day of work, Tonya and I cleaned the shelves together. We only finished two shelves, then she sent me home. The following day, I started my training in the kitchen. The kitchen manager gave me a hat that I had to wear all the time while working in the kitchen. She showed me where to get my apron and hairnet and asked me to wear them. "We're not allowed to use a cellphone while on duty and no jewelry," she said.

I just nodded while tying my apron at the back of my waist. She introduced me to my coworkers, including a guy who asked if he could touch my black hair because he'd never touched someone's real black hair before. He looked nice and funny, but I found his request creepy. I just smiled at him, tied my hair into a bun, and put on the hairnet and my new hat.

There were three ladies working in the kitchen that day—two of them were busy making pizza, and the other lady was standing at the sub sandwich station making an order for a customer. The kitchen manager wanted me to stand next to the ladies that were making pizza and watch them. "Do you really have to count how many pepperonis you have to put on there?" I asked one lady who was looking at the paper that was taped on the wall, right above the pizza station. It listed all the measurements and how much meat—including the pieces of pepperoni—to put on a small, medium, or large size pizza.

My coworker said yes because she didn't want to be in trouble.

"I don't do that shit," the lady who was making sandwiches said, "unless the area supervisor is around because she's so meticulous."

A few minutes later, I stood next to her to watch her make sandwiches. She was showing me the procedure, where to get the liner, the cheese, the bread, and everything. I also helped them prepare lunch by getting the containers for cheeseburgers ready and slicing the whole pizzas and putting them in the warmer.

Once I got home, I sat down on the recliner and rested my feet up in the air. It was not easy to stand for six straight hours. They told me I could take a short break, but there were no available chairs in the kitchen to sit on and no break room inside the store. I sat inside my car for a few minutes, then went back inside the store after I saw more customers coming in.

I met another coworker who'd been working there for a couple years, and she trained me. But I tried to hide behind the food rack that was covered by big white plastic—where we put the trays of donuts and bread—when I saw a few people I knew in town. I didn't know why I was feeling shy. I hoped, I would get over the feeling of embarrassment.

My coworker walked me through the kitchen and showed me where to find everything—the condiments, tongs, pizza flour, sandwiches, meats, donuts, and whatnot. Then we went inside the freezer, and she showed me where to find the crumbled eggs, meat, hamburger patties, donuts, chicken strips, etc. I was amazed at how they stacked and organized the small freezer. They made everything fit in there. My coworker said she did it, and she was the one who put things away on delivery day.

They only trained me for a week. I showed up at six o'clock in the morning so that the donut maker who worked overnight could go home, and another coworker would replace her to help me prepare breakfast. We served hash browns, biscuits and gravy, breakfast sandwiches, and breakfast pizza, which I found odd the first time I saw it because in the Philippines, I never had or saw a pizza with cheese sauce, scrambled eggs, bacon or sausage crumbles, and mozzarella cheese on top. But I could tell a lot of customers liked it because I had to make a pan of sausage or bacon breakfast pizza every twenty minutes. I could also make a pizza or sandwich by myself with a little help from a coworker, except when there was a line of customers ordering a sandwich.

It got busy before 11 a.m., when customers were still coming and we had to keep up with the food warmer, making sure they didn't run out of pizza or sandwiches. I was still learning how to make a pizza without messing up the sides or putting a hole in the center. *This should be simple, and here I am taking forever to make a perfect pizza dough,* I thought. But it got easier the more I made them. A one-topping pizza was the easiest to make, but nothing would be easier than when a customer ordered a pizza without pizza sauce.

I also got confused when making a beef or a sausage pizza. My coworker saw me making a beef pizza order, but I put on sausage crumbles. "Beef is the darker meat, and sausage is the lighter meat," my coworker explained. We also had to fill the donut case, swap containers for sub and pizza stations, then wash those containers when we were not busy, and before we went home, we had to stock water, soda, milk, and different brands of juices, kid's drinks, and Gatorade in the cooler, and take empty crates outside when we were done. I tried to do this as fast as I could so that I could go home.

I met new coworkers, and two of them were arguing about if I was an Asian or not. One coworker insisted I was not, because I was a Filipino. Some coworkers asked about the Philippines—the weather, if we got snow there, if it was close to the Atlantic

Ocean, if we played football there, if we had schools there. "Do you eat goats or monkey brain there? Or worship cows?" one person asked.

We had a new coworker named Rhonda who was in her fifties. Rhonda liked to talk and she told me she was a breast cancer survivor. I liked working with her because we talked about a lot of things, like motherhood and some unfortunate decisions she made in life. Weeks later, Rhonda told me her cancer had come back, and she had to quit her job because of her doctor's advice. I saw her one afternoon at a restaurant in Fremont, and she told me about her surgery. I gave her a hug and told her I'd keep her in my prayers, but I haven't seen her since then.

꠵

After doing the same routine at the convenience store, I decided to start a blog called "The Pinay Mom: A Filipina Mom's Simple Living," where I wrote about my simple life in America. Writing was one of my hobbies, and that was something I was always excited about every time I got home from work.

꠵

The managers came up to me in the kitchen one busy morning and asked me if I would be interested in making donuts. "We will train you as soon as you say yes," they said. "The donut maker is having a problem with her child, and she might call in more often." A coworker that was working with me that day warned me not to do it because I would end up doing it more often. "I'm sure of it," she said. "They asked me many times, but I always say no to them." The kitchen manager told her "Shh!" trying to tell her not to discourage me.

Another coworker told me she wouldn't trade her sleep for fifty cents an hour because it was not worth it. But instead of listening to my two coworkers, I told the managers I would try and let them know if I liked it or not. They told me there was a donut helper who came in at three o'clock in the morning on weekends, and she was a great help.

⌇

I was watching Karla, the donut maker, put a brown liner on each cookie sheet that we had laid out on the long prep table. She told me this was the first thing she did when she started her shift. After she was done putting liner on twenty-five trays, she gave me a pen and the production schedule planner that was on the clipboard and asked me to count all the unsold donuts in the donut case and write them down. I told Karla I was done counting all of them, and she said "Put a dozen donuts with holes in a box, put the **"DAY OLD DONUT"** sticker on it, and throw any leftovers in the trash."

I felt bad throwing away leftover donuts, like when we'd throw away pizza or any food in the warmer that was sitting for more than an hour. I knew there were some people out there who were starving, yet I was throwing away food that should've been given to them. I wished the store would do something to avoid wasting food by giving it to shelters or not making too much. Karla told me there was a lady who scavenged boxes of day-old donuts from the store's dumpster and gave them away to other people, but she said the store was just following the state law.

Karla asked me to soak the donut trays in the sink, and we would wash them later. She showed me how to set the oven temperature, and we started making two pans of pizza. She said we had to serve every hour because there were a few customers who would stop by. We put one pan in the oven while we put the other one in the prep refrigerator for later. Then we started going back and forth from the freezer to get different boxes of donuts and started panning up.

I wrote down everything that Karla taught me that night, like how many donuts to make, the oven temperature for flips, cookies, and mini-cookies. "We have to decorate cookies on Halloween, Thanksgiving, Valentine's Day, and Christmas," she said. But I didn't think I would do that. It was time consuming. I would just put a smiley face or sprinkles on them to make it easier. We had to finish everything before we went home. We had to finish our dishes and swap frosting containers.

I slept all morning when I got home after doing the donut shift. Tim watched the girls that morning and let me sleep until noon. Friday night was busy. I always got a few pizza or sandwich orders while I was running trays of donuts to and from the oven. There were interesting customers that came in during those hours. One customer took a picture of me while I was making his burrito, and another customer gave me a six-dollar tip for making his sandwich. I always got behind, but I was thankful that the donut helper made my work easier. She washed trays for me when she had time, and I didn't have to help her prepare breakfast at four in the morning.

That shift was on and off. A lot of the time I worked in the kitchen at my morning shift, but every time Karla called in sick, I covered for her. But I noticed that I'd been working three weekends in a row now, and they only gave me a weekend off when I asked about it. The area supervisor came to the store to train managers and donut makers on how to make donuts because, obviously, we'd been doing it wrong. "This is your 'bible' to follow," the area supervisor said while holding the food manual which showed us the procedures, measurements, water temperatures, and everything. I had no problem following the 'bible' if we got enough help in the kitchen.

⤬

Around Christmas time, I noticed I was losing hours when our schedule came out. One week I only got twenty hours. I asked the manager who did the scheduling and told her I needed more than twenty hours a week. "Since we're closing on Christmas Eve, we took care of the full-time employees first by giving them the minimum hours they need to keep the full-time status. The next time the schedule rolls out, you'll get the same hours like before," she promised.

I then noticed a change on my weekend hours; I had to start working at eight o'clock in the morning instead of six. I went back to the manager again and asked about it, but she told me the kitchen manager came up to her and said it was me who wanted it. I told her I never talked to the kitchen manager about it. The following week, she changed my schedule. Then they asked me if I would like to work as a full-time donut maker because Karla was quitting. They said I would work at least thirty-five hours a week. I accepted it because they promised me I'd be back to my morning shift once they found a new donut maker, and I would still keep my full-time status.

A few months later, I'd trained ten donut makers—most of them didn't last long. Some quit while others got fired. One guy just walked out at midnight, an hour after his shift started, because he was not too happy with everything. Another donut maker told me he couldn't say he was proud of this job because he used to paint trucks. Not too long after, he got fired.

I always ended up doing the donut maker shift except on a "truck day," when I had to help put away boxes of donuts, bags of pizza and donut flour, frozen meat, and cheese. My back hurt every time I put away heavy boxes of pizza sauce cans. We had to stack boxes and date everything—every box, each meat package, fruit salad in a cup, etc. It was a lot of work between preparing food and doing this at the same time when there were only three of us in the kitchen.

Going back and forth from inside the freezer was always not fun. It was below zero degrees inside when I had to organize the freezer. I wore my thick brown coat, put the hood on top of my hat to cover my ears, and wore thick gloves. The top shelves were hard to do. I had to move the boxes that had older dates on top of the new boxes that had just gotten delivered. After I put everything away that needed to go in the freezer, I did the walk-in cooler next where we stocked boxes of mozzarella cheese, meat for sandwiches, pizza dough, and salad.

The managers told me that corporate wanted us, the donut makers, to clean the kitchen first before we started making donuts. I told them it was not happening because it was not possible to get everything done—washing trays, change the frosting containers, bag donut dough mix and put peanut butter crispy bites and puppy chow in a cup—unless we extended working for another hour, which they didn't want to happen because of overtime.

∽

A year passed, and I was still doing the donut maker shift most of the time. There were weeks or month when I didn't make donuts, but they always put me back again because the donut maker quit or got fired. The job was getting old.

We were short on help and sometimes there was not enough time to do what they asked us to do, like making more bread or sandwiches. One day, a coworker left dishes in the sink because she got so busy in the kitchen; while another coworker ignored a coworker who had passed out on the kitchen floor. "I was too busy going back and forth from the freezer to get ready for lunch," my coworker reasoned out.

Tonya got promoted, and we got a new manager, Kathy. I told Kathy I was looking for another job because I was really burned-out. She offered to let me work at the cash register to see if it worked out for me. I agreed, hoping the change would keep me from quitting.

My first day at the cash register was overwhelming. A coworker was teaching me how to do certain paperwork and count the bundled coins in the safe before she started teaching me how to run the cash register. She also showed me how to process check payments and sell lottery tickets while there was a line of customers. That day, I didn't remember anything except finding the button to push in front of the machine. But a customer gave me a dollar tip when he found out it was my first day working the cash register.

The cash register people had to mop the floor, clean restrooms, pick up trash inside and outside the store, and do the cigarette and lottery inventory while the overnight cash register person cleaned the coffee machine and the tea maker. My new cashier job was completely different from working in the kitchen. My coworker who was training me said, "I like doing the cash register because I use my brain to run the machine, unlike in the kitchen, where you don't."

I tried to memorize where on the rack I would find each cigarette brand and type. It was embarrassing when a customer told me how to find their pack of cigarettes. Some of them would say, "On your right." "On your left." "Oh, you missed it!" "No, the next one." "There; you got it!" while I was standing on the small ladder finding their cigarettes.

For a short time, we had to ask every customer for a dollar donation for a good cause, but some customers whined about it. One customer said he preferred donating locally because some corporations ask for donations as a "business." "The people on top get the money and not the promised recipients. It's a scam," he added.

My managers still made me work donut shifts on truck days and on weekdays, and it was getting frustrating. Kathy told me to "hang in there" because the store was short on help. But I told her, "If this keeps going, I'll get another job."

And I did.

The Custodian

By the end of January 2015, the school superintendent asked Tim if I would be interested in working at the school. I'd met the school superintendent, Dr. Seaton, at the convenience store when he was picking up his pizza order one morning, and it was interesting that he thought of offering me a job. Tim gave me Dr. Seaton's phone number so that I could call him, which I did the following day.

"What kind of job offer do you have for me, Dr. Seaton?" I asked.

"Well," Dr. Seaton started, "it's not really a job offer."

I'd asked Tim the night before what job he thought Dr. Seaton would offer me. He said, "Probably a cleaning job." And he was right.

Dr. Seaton said, "We're looking for part-time help to clean the school if there's a game or a school event—at whatever time would work for you." We set up a time to talk more about it.

"You can work twenty-five hours a week," Dr. Seaton started our conversation the afternoon I met him at the school's conference room. "You can do things like vacuuming classrooms or picking up things off the floor, as long as we keep the school clean," he said.

He was aware that we had two daughters whom we didn't want to take to daycare, and he was willing to work with our schedules. Then he took out his cellphone from his pocket and called the school secretary; he asked her to bring over an application form. The secretary came in the room a few seconds later and she handed me the two-page form. I read the big bold words that said: "**Non-Certificated Application For Employment.**" I felt awkward filling out the form in front of the two of them. They were all quiet and they were watching me until I finished filling out the application form.

"So, you're from the Philippines," Dr. Seaton asked while reading my application.

"Yes, I am," I answered.

He mentioned my college degree, clerical skills, and blogging that I listed under the "Activities" category, which I knew would be unnecessary for the job he was offering me; I wouldn't use any of those there.

I accepted the job without asking how much I would get paid. I didn't know why I didn't have the courage to ask, but I already had an idea because Tim had been working there for three years as a full-time custodian, and he was offered $11.50 an hour as a starting pay. I thought I might get less than that since I would only be part-time, but that would still be my highest starting pay rate since I'd started working in America.

The secretary asked for my driver's license so that she could make a copy of it. Dr. Seaton and I were left in the conference room, and he asked me to save the maintenance director's phone number. I didn't have my cellphone with me to save the number or have a piece of paper to write it down, but I was glad I had a pen with me. I had no choice but to take out the small book that was in my purse.

"What are you reading?" Dr. Seaton curiously asked, looking at the book I was holding.

"Maybe You Should Write a Book," I told him while showing him the front cover. The book's author was Ralph Daigh. "I started reading it a few days ago."

"Oh," Dr. Seaton said, nodding. He told me I could start showing up for work whatever time I wanted to, or as early as 5:15 in the morning, if it worked for me. I told him I had no problem with that, but it would depend on my schedule from the convenience store. "But on my day off I can work on that hour and I can still work after I do my overnight donut shift. We'll see how it goes," I told him. He said that was fine.

The secretary came back with my driver's license, and Dr. Seaton asked me to follow him so that I could meet the maintenance director. After I met the maintenance director, Dr. Seaton walked me through the new school gym and told me I could do things like sweep the floor or pick up whatever I saw on the floor. Between my job at the convenience store and this part-time cleaning job, I'd be working at least sixty hours a week; Tim warned me to "take it easy."

I'd never done a cleaning job for a living in my whole life, besides helping out my aunt one summer when I was a teenager by doing household chores or pulling grasses in the front yard. I knew this job at the school would be interesting. "I'm not going to say I love and am really excited about it, but this job pays higher than my two previous jobs and works out really well on our schedule." I said to Tim. I didn't have to work on weird hours or work on weekends. For some people 5:15 a.m. was too early, but I was used to it.

꙰

It was my day off at the convenience store, and I decided to work at the school. I arrived a few minutes early and parked in the school's parking lot at the back, where Dr. Seaton told me to park. I didn't have a key to get in the building, but a couple minutes later, another car pulled up. I got out my car and I introduced myself to Nancy when she got out of her car. Nancy said, "We'll be working together."

When we got into the maintenance office, Nancy gave me my timesheet, which was on the clipboard, and asked me to write down my time. Then she handed me a set of keys with a keychain ring that said "Extra Custodian" on it. She told me which key I'd use to get in to every classroom so that I could start vacuuming. "Except the science lab, art room, and industrial room that need to be swept," Nancy said. The school building was big, and Nancy gave me a printout of the school map on long bond paper for a guide. She said, "Some rooms are messy because they have not been vacuumed for a few days since the custodian you replaced quit." At this school, teachers and students started showing up before 7:30 a.m., but there were a few students who came earlier. They either sat in the cafeteria, reading or talking, or sat on the bench, killing time until the bell rang. One teacher came to work before 6:30 a.m. I asked her why she was so early. She said, "I've been doing this for many years. I like it because it's quiet and there are no distractions and I get more things done."

One thing I noticed about the school was that the students and teachers didn't wear a school I.D. or a uniform, like we did at every public or private school in the Philippines. The students didn't call their teachers ma'am or sir. They called them mister, missus, or miss, and I didn't know how I should address the teachers—as the students called them, or just by their first names.

That morning, I picked up crumpled papers, pens, pencils, fake nails with orange and silver polish, candy wrappers, and jelly beans off the floor before I vacuumed a few classrooms.

I didn't finish all the classrooms before the bell rang at 8:05 a.m. Nancy asked me to clean the trophy cases, which took me at least a couple hours to finish. Before I went home, I got a small pink card with a lollipop taped inside, thanking me for being a part of the school. Before I left, I told Nancy what day I'd come back to work, which would be in the next couple days, since I had to work at the convenience store.

The next morning I showed up, Nancy told me I could sweep the art room after the bell rang because it was the art teacher's planning period. The room was full of creativity and had tons of books on the shelves. When we had our art subject in elementary in the Philippines, we didn't have all these things. The only art projects I remembered doing were making the color wheel and carving something out of a big potato. We had to pay more attention to our teacher, who would give quizzes anytime. We focused more on books, tests, quizzes, recitation, and class participation when we took our art class.

I met the art teacher for the first time when he came into his room while I was sweeping the floor. I introduced myself, and he did the same. He seemed so nice and easy to talk to. Somehow, our conversation ended up with me telling him that I was originally from the Philippines and married to an American. He asked one of the questions I got a lot, if I married someone from the service. I said no. He said his two grandfathers were stationed in the Philippines during World War II.

The next time I went to his classroom, he brought a small box that his two grandfathers brought from the Philippines. He wanted to tell me more about them. There were a few things in the box and a small photo album with black and white, post-war pictures that one of his grandfathers took. I'd never seen pictures like those, the aftermath of the war. In the box, there were shells and other Filipino native products, including a hula coconut bra that women wore at the dance festival. I told him we had a lot of festivals in the Philippines.

Every time I went to his room, we talked for a little bit, and I told him how artistic he was with all the artwork he had in his room. He told me the meaning behind the Spain flag, what the coat of arms meant, and where the dollar sign came from, and he showed me the royal family's ancestry tree picture that he'd made and had hanging on the wall. It looked like he'd put a lot of effort into doing it. He was one of the most interesting people I'd met at the school.

Most of the time, I worked at the school three or four days a week. I tried to work after my overnight donut shift, but that made me really tired every time I went home. Tim called me a few times because I'd napped too long and missed picking up Marie from preschool. So, I gave my resignation at the convenience store, but Kathy asked me if I could work part-time and see how I liked it. I said, "No. I make the same amount of money just by working part-time at the school, and I won't get tired all the time by working different hours every week."

It was a bittersweet decision quitting the convenience store job. I met a lot of customers; some of them gave me a hard time, but I ended up knowing them well. I wouldn't forget a customer who showed me her mastectomy by pulling her shirt down one night. She told me she had breast cancer and her doctor told her she only had a few months to live. The last time I saw her, she came in past midnight, and I noticed she'd gained weight. She said it was because of her medications. Before she left the store that night, she said goodbye to me, and she never came back after that. Her daughter told me that she was already bedridden and couldn't get around; shortly after, that lady passed away.

I also made a sandwich for a customer a week before she got into a car accident, but luckily, she survived. Months after that, another customer whom I made sandwiches for a couple times also got into an accident and died. In that frustrating job, I got the chance to meet those special people and talk to them while I made their pizza or sandwiches. When I found out their unfortunate fates, how could I forget them?

⌒

I called Dr. Seaton and told him I was interested in working full-time that school year if there was an opening. He said we would talk about it later. Right away, I changed my work schedule at the school. I decided to show up to work at 6 a.m. and work until

11 a.m., Monday through Friday, making my twenty-five hours a week. I did the same routine everyday: vacuum a few classrooms first, sweep the art room, vacuum the entryways, wipe the windows and ledges, clean the weight room twice a week, and clean each student's locker to wipe off some writings, scratches, or shoe marks—some were easy to get off, while some didn't come off at all.

One morning I told a student, "No kicking!" when I saw him closing his locker using his foot, but he just looked at me and smiled. "It's karate!" he mumbled while heading back to his classroom.

Nancy showed me how she cleaned the restrooms because she was taking a day off. "Would you mind doing it while I'm gone?" she asked.

I told her I didn't mind at all because it didn't look hard to do. I just had to spray disinfectant in the sink, then spray a bowl cleaner in the toilet. I also had to put a new roll of paper towels in the dispenser. I almost puked when I went to the men's restroom because of the smell coming from the urinals. I sprayed disinfectant in each urinal bowl, holding my breath, until that awful smell faded away. "I don't know how you do it every day, but I commend you for doing this every morning, five days a week." I told Nancy.

I noticed a lot of nice things in the school. It had a nice library where students could use computers for free. When I was a high school student at the public school in Daet, we had to pay fifty pesos (almost a dollar equivalent) every month for a computer laboratory fee; paying that fee was a struggle for some students, including me. Because of the limited number of computers, we also had to share the computer with three or four classmates. I found out the students could also borrow a laptop from the American school and take it home so that they could do their school projects or homework. In the Philippines, you either had to borrow a laptop from someone or go to an internet café and pay a rental fee to have it.

The Philippines public schools couldn't compete with the big gym they had at that school I worked at, which had complete facilities. It was also interesting to know that this school provided art supplies, calculators, protractors, etc. for students to borrow. We never had those in our public school in the Philippines, and we didn't have a few school custodians around. We only had one custodian in high school, and just like in Japan, students cleaned the classroom. We swept and scrubbed the floor without help from a janitor.

We didn't have Special Ed teachers or paraprofessional teachers either. But I wondered why the school didn't have a flag ceremony every morning to sing the National Anthem, Patriotic Oath, and the Patriotic song, like we did in the Philippines. We exercised after that too. As a country where that majority were Catholic, we had a Religion subject in elementary and Values Education in high school as part of the school curriculum.

One morning, a teacher was in disbelief when I knocked on his door. "Did you just knock?" he asked. "No one ever knocks on my door, even the staff, they just all come in."

"Knocking was something we learned from our Values Education subject because our teacher said it was a sign of respect to someone's privacy, regardless if the door was closed or not." I told him. "I always knock because I don't want to surprise or scare someone, and it's always the right thing to do."

The classrooms in America were not crowded either because the teacher to student ratio was not bad. In the Philippines, there were over forty students in one classroom that had no air conditioner, only a ceiling or a stand fan if the students contributed money to buy it. Books were limited too, and we had to share with our classmates.

American public schools got bonds so that they could use the money for school projects, while bonds don't exist at Philippine public schools. If a school wanted to build something like a gym or a library or a classroom, they'd have to raise funds by soliciting from politicians, which was frustrating a lot of times. If there was another project, like funding a school club, the students did a beauty contest or sent each candidate a bundle of small white envelopes to give to their families, friends, and people who were willing to donate money. Whoever raised the highest amount of money won a trophy, a gift, and a sash. The runner-up also got a trophy, but not as tall as the winner's trophy. These were some differences that I saw between the schools in the different countries, and it made me sad to think that my native country hadn't taken the American schools as their model so that Filipino children could get the best and comfortable education they deserved.

I started working as a custodian in February, and then the school year was almost over. I'd been only working there for three months, and I told Tim, "I got bored cleaning and I'm sure doing this in the summer would be no different, or worse, more boring. I'm not sure how long I will stay here." But every time, I thought of the money we saved by both working there. I wanted to keep that job for that reason, "But I'll see what happens next." I said. The monotony of the job bored me, so I found another part-time job as a local coordinator with foreign exchange students.

Exchange Student Representative

I was happy to get a response a day after I submitted my job application online for the position of "area representative for exchange students" in Fremont. I had an online meeting with the manager and did my training with her, where I learned about the organization's background and my responsibilities. My job was to place the exchange students, coordinate with the school, follow up on the student's visa—or, as they called it, the I-20 form—and find volunteer families to host them for the entire school year. My pay would be based on how many students I placed. It was not much, but it looked like fun.

To do this job, I had to be a certified local coordinator and I had to take another online training class, where I learned about the codes for federal regulations, public diplomacy, and the rules for exchange visitor programs. I passed the test, and my certification was good for one year. I did this job every afternoon, right after I got off work from the school. I called a few businesses in nearby towns to drop off flyers. I got responses, but no positive answers in the end. Some said they couldn't do it at that time because they were busy remodeling their houses, and one mother said, "I can't wait for my son to move out, so why have another one? Ha ha ha."

I still had to work at 6:00 a.m. at the school, and it was weird working there in the summer—not seeing students walking around the hallways or sitting at the cafeteria. The silence and working eight hours made the day longer. We had to deep clean everything. The tables and chairs in every classroom needed to be wiped down, the carpets needed to be shampooed, the floors needed to be stripped and coated, and we had to do any other cleaning duties that we couldn't do during the school year. Nancy asked me to clean every student's locker; there were over three hundred of them. I found Biology books that I gave to the secretary and sweaters and pants that I put in the lost and found bin. I wondered why students would leave those things.

I took home magnets, pencils, notebooks, pens, binders, markers, and rulers after cleaning the lockers out for two weeks. Then I started wiping tables, plastic trash cans, chairs, boards, drawers, and ledges in every classroom while Nancy vacuumed and shampooed the carpet. After we were done cleaning all the classrooms, we started cleaning the restrooms by scrubbing every sink and urinal. Then we wiped the bathroom stall dividers and handles.

That time of the year, I only had to clean the weight room once a week, and that was every Friday, when it got really dirty. I started cleaning the office area, wiping the trophy cases, and vacuuming entryways afterwards. Between cleaning and working my new part-time job, I was tired all the time, but I had to keep both jobs because one was a steady paycheck that helped us pay our bills and the other one kept me away from boredom, even though it sometimes took a few weeks to find volunteer families.

⌒

Dr. Seaton offered me a full-time custodial position. But I told him, "I'm not sure because I'm already bored by just doing this job as part-time. So how much more when I do it full-time?"

"Just to break your routine, you can try to be a bus driver," Dr. Seaton suggested. "You'll drive in the morning, then do the cleaning after that." He also offered to let me ride with someone in a bus for a year so I could see how they do it and if I would like it. "Also," he said "the benefits are something you can't refuse."

They offered free health and life insurance, five-day vacation leave, ten-day sick leave, and two days of personal leave—all starting on my first day of work as a full-time custodian. I accepted his offer, and I signed a contract before the school year started. My new schedule was from 5:15 a.m. to 1:15 p.m., Monday through Friday.

The school gave their custodians five free uniform shirts. I picked collarless shirts with different colors: orange, pink, gray, white, and light blue. They all had my name embroidered on the left corner and the school's name on top.

The month of August arrived so quickly; suddenly it was my first day of work as a full-time custodian, and in a couple weeks, the teachers and students would be back. I realized I would never forget my first day there, not because it was my first day of full-time work, but because I hurt my foot early in the morning. I missed one step as I was going down our backdoor stairs while heading to work. I could barely hit the pedal to drive my car. My foot swelled up at work, and I could barely walk straight. I was on crutches and missed work for a couple days.

The following days, we were busy finishing everything. The students would start in a few days, but first we were having a staff report meeting in the cafeteria. Dr. Seaton introduced the new employees—including me—before he presented the school plans for the year. It was nice to know everybody and have them know my name. The custodians also had another meeting that day to talk about our plans and duties for that school year. I would be picking up the trash from each classroom every morning, vacuuming the middle school classrooms and entryways, cleaning the weight room twice a week, and Nancy and I would clean the cafeteria.

It was back to school time, and the first week felt weird working eight hours a day. I always kept myself busy by doing my job, including cleaning the cafeteria. There was a reserved table where some teachers, other staff, and custodians ate together. Nancy and I started a system for cleaning the cafeteria where I swept the big chunks of food and crumbs left on the table, then wiped them with a wet rag while Nancy swept the floor. Then we mopped the floor.

⌒

A lady left a voicemail on my cellphone one afternoon after I got home from working at the school saying she was interested in hosting a foreign exchange student. The lady found the information from her pastor, who got one of my private messages on their church Facebook page. It had been a couple weeks since school started, yet my exchange students were still in their home countries, waiting for their placements.

I visited the couple's home a day later for the orientation. They needed to sign papers, and I had to take some pictures of their house as part of the screening process. They were both retired and had gone on a mission trip abroad a few years prior. I told them, "I also have another student that needs placement." I was so happy when they decided to host that student too. The two students arrived, and I gave them an orientation. As their Area Representative, I had to check with them every month to see if there were any issues at the school or with their host parents and if they had any questions.

⌒

I had just barely been working as a full-time custodian for a month and I wanted to quit or reduce my hours, at least. A couple teachers asked me if I liked working there. I just said, "I do because people are nice and there's no drama, unlike what I'd seen at the convenience store." But doing the same cleaning routine every day or walking around the hallways to find something else to do was more boring. The staff, the teachers, my fellow custodians, and the students were nice, but I didn't find any excitement in doing that job. There was always something missing—the challenge or satisfaction. I didn't think I was going to last there. Just like my first day of working here, I was asking myself, *How long I will stay here?*

Becoming a U.S. Citizen

I applied for my U.S. citizenship in March of 2015, did my fingerprinting in April, and had my interview in June. Some friends and coworkers asked about my immigration. They wanted to know how long it took me to get my citizenship and how much it cost. I said, "When Tim and I started filing for my immigration papers, between filing fees and other costs, I could tell it was expensive." But my interview with Miss Davis at the Immigration Services in Omaha sufficed those costs.

Once we got into the Immigration Services building in Omaha, I noticed a Somalian lady and some fellow Asians sitting in the waiting area, waiting for their names to be called. I dropped off my appointment notice in the drop box at the reception desk, and we found a seat across from a lady wearing a *hijab*, and rocking a car seat that's in front of her. She said her baby was only a few weeks old. Marie and Olivia kept peeking and told the lady that her baby was cute. She asked me where I came from. "From the Philippines," I said. She was from Somalia and lived two hours away from Omaha. "I work with some Filipinos at the packing plant," she said.

We were still talking when my name was called by the immigration officer, Miss Davis, who had a jolly face, like a sun smiling at you. She seemed very friendly compared to the immigration officer who interviewed me a few years ago for my permanent residency. Tim and the girls stayed in the waiting area. Miss Davis and I started talking while we headed to her office. I told her about our detours because we missed our turn coming here: "We thought we would be late but we still made it on time."

Miss Davis asked me to put down my things—folders and purse—on the vacant chair next to my chair once we got to her office. She asked me to remain standing and raise my right hand, and just like when on trial, Miss Davis asked me to swear to tell truth. Then we both sat down, and Miss Davis asked me to verify my name, my address, and my date of birth.

"Are you ready for your tests?" Miss Davis asked me with a smile on her face. I told her, "I'm nervous." But she assured me that I would be fine. To pass the citizenship test, I had to take a civic, speaking, writing, and reading test. They said the speaking test was done during the conversation with the immigration officer. *Maybe that was why Miss Davis kept on talking to me from the beginning,* I thought. "We'll do the civic test first," Miss Davis said. They'd sent me home with a civic test booklet when I came to the Immigration Services building last April for my fingerprinting (biometrics). The booklet had one hundred questions with key answers. I had to answer six questions correctly out of ten. I read it over and over again, just like how I'd studied my driver's manual a few years prior. *I would really feel bad if I failed today,* I thought before we started.

"Ready?" Miss Davis asked.

I smiled at her and said, "I'm ready."

"How many amendments does the Constitution have?"

"Twenty-seven," I answered.

"Who makes federal laws?"

"Congress."

"What is the name of the Vice President of the United States now?"

"Joseph R. Biden, Jr."

"What is the highest court in the United States?"

"Supreme Court."

"What group of people was taken to America and sold as slaves?"

"Africans."

"Why did the colonists fight the British?"

"Because of high taxes," I said.

Miss Davis nodded and smiled. Then she showed me a piece of paper with three sentences written on it.

"Pick one sentence you want to read," Miss Davis said.

I picked the sentence that said, "I can vote."

Then she gave me a blank piece of paper, and asked me to pick one sentence I wanted to write. I chose the same sentence and wrote it on the paper.

"Congratulations!" Miss Davis said while shaking my hand. "You're a U.S. citizen now." Both of us stood up, and she told me I'd be getting a notice in the mail about the time and place for my naturalization ceremony. Then she walked with me, heading out the door, where I saw Tim and our daughters waiting for me. Tim was smiling but really surprised.

"That quick?" Tim asked.

I said, "Yes, and I passed the citizenship test!"

He was so happy for me and told me "Congratulations."

We decided to go to China Buffet to celebrate.

Tim called our local newspaper and told them about my citizenship, and they wanted to write an article about my journey to citizenship. "They've never done this kind of story in this town," a man from the paper said. Dr. Seaton was happy for me and told me I was the example of the American Dream.

Three months after that interview, we headed to Homestead National Monument of America in Beatrice, Nebraska, to attend my citizenship ceremony. I was wearing a knee-length ivory lace dress with a pink tiny belt that I bought from JC Penney. It was an expensive fifty-dollar dress, but I didn't mind paying that price because I'd be using it for one of the most special days of my life in the country that welcomed me seven years ago.

Once we got to the Homestead National Monument of America, they asked us, the immigrants who would be taking an oath, to fall in line so that we could sign our names on the sign-in sheet. We had to surrender our green cards and the letter we received from the Immigration Services. It was amazing to see all of the immigrants with different faces, skin colors, and countries of origin, all smiling and happy. Some of my fellow immigrants were wearing their traditional clothing. There were at least forty immigrants in the line, and they gave each one of us a big white envelope that had a couple booklets, pamphlets, a small American flag, a signed letter from President Obama congratulating us, and the ceremony program in it.

I read The Citizen's Almanac booklet while we waited for the program to start. It told a brief American history, the background of the Declaration of Independence, the Immigration in 1800s, and the presidents that made this country great. It made me smile to read the article about Franklin D. Roosevelt, my favorite U.S. president. His name was popular in my native country because of his great contribution to the Philippine independence. Some streets and highways in Manila were named after him.

Just looking around the beautiful courtyard and seeing the smiles and excitement on my fellow immigrants' faces, I wonder what kind of stories they had and how they ended up here. Did they come over here just like I did—answering a phone call from a customer complaining about his bill and marrying him less than a year later? A lot of people told me it was fate how Tim and I met.

I talked to a couple fellow immigrants and some of them were just like me; they married an American. I was sure not all of us had the same process of immigration. I found out that some got petitioned by their parents or family members or some came over as refugees. We sat on the bench under the tree next to a family of four. I noticed the daughter's black t-shirt with a long statement on the back about the massacre that happened in South Sudan in 2013. I was not sure if they were refugees or not, but I knew there were some immigrants who had that kind of story—full of pain and misery. Some of them might have seen terrible things before coming over to America.

I talked to the daughter, who was in her twenties. She said they were from Sudan and her father was getting naturalized. They'd been living in the U.S. for ten years, but her father couldn't pass the English test when he applied for citizenship before. "But we're all happy today because in a few hours, my father, just like you, will be holding that piece of American citizenship certificate." she said.

Every time someone asked me how much it cost me—or cost us—to come over to America, I didn't know what the right answer was, once we'd listened to other people's stories. It was priceless to those who'd seen terror and devastation in their homelands.

They asked all of the immigrants to find our seats because the program was starting shortly. For me, it was a solemn and moving ceremony, listening to the judge and guest speakers. The judge asked us to remain seated while we were taking an oath because it was hot out. He didn't want us to be tired. Raising our right hands, we repeated after him, saying the Pledge of Allegiance to America. Then they asked us to fall in line and they started calling our names and saying the countries we came from. They shook our hands and gave us our naturalization certificates. I was just thankful to be where I was that day with my family and my fellow immigrants on September 15, 2015, becoming U.S. citizens.

The school celebrated my citizenship a day later. They had a big cake decorated with the American flag for me. I got flowers, angel food cake, cards, and a huge blanket with "USA" printed on it. We had a citizenship party at home the next weekend; my Filipino and American friends showed up, including our neighbors Bob and Doris. We served hamburgers, chicken, and Filipino food. I got more cards and gifts. I kept all of these things—the presents, the newspaper article about my citizenship, and the pictures—in my memory box.

Two weeks later, we went to the Social Security Administration office in Omaha to update my immigration status from a green card holder to a

U.S. citizen. And that same week, I also registered to vote and applied for a U.S. passport because we were planning to take a vacation to the Philippines the next summer.

Second Philippine Vacation

One school year passed, and I was doing the same cleaning routine—show up at 5:15 a.m., vacuum classrooms, clean the cafeteria Monday through Friday, clean the weight room on Wednesdays and Fridays, wipe the glass windows, sweep the hallway floors. But I didn't become a bus driver. I was also busy working my other job—meeting with my exchange students and finding prospective host families for the next school year. It was a lot of work, but I enjoyed it, and summer break arrived fast.

Tim and I decided to visit my family in the Philippines for the second time because it'd been three years since we went back there. I knew my family would enjoy Marie and Olivia even more because they'd started to talk a lot, like chatter boxes. Dr. Seaton let us take a three-week vacation, and we were using what we had left on our vacation leave days, but Tim had to cancel his plane ticket because he got terminated when the school year was over. "You will enjoy and spend more time with your family if I'm not around," Tim suggested.

But before we went to the Philippines, I told Dr. Seaton I planned on quitting. "I'm not going to renew my contract," I said to him one morning. I thought it was better to let Dr. Seaton know in the summer so that he could hire someone before the school year started. He asked, "Does this have anything to do with Tim's termination?"

I told him, "I already planned on this months before. I got bored working here and I can't see myself doing this again for another year. I'm planning to pursue my writing career."

He said, "We'll talk once you get back from vacation."

∽

"Why you're not coming?" Marie asked Tim while we were about to check-in at the airport. I could tell Tim was sad hearing that question, even though we'd already told them many times that Daddy was not coming with us. Still, it seemed they never understood. Instead, Tim told them he'd stay home to watch our house and clean it.

"Okay" Marie said while hugging Tim's leg. Tim took his cellphone out and took pictures. The first shot was the three of them; then just me and the girls. Having a U.S. passport made this trip easier. There was no hassle like the first time we went to the

Philippines; they didn't ask for a visa or any other paperwork for me to get out of the country. But who would have thought traveling alone with two young daughters—Marie was five and Olivia was four— would be easier.

Both of them walked with me inside the airport to find our plane gate, but too much walking inside the O'Hare International Airport in Chicago was tiring for both of them. Between walking and riding a tram, I wished Tim hadn't cancelled his ticket. I would've rather had him helping me with the girls. Olivia almost got left at the tram station, where she stepped back at the closing door. I was holding their hands, but Olivia got scared. I blocked the closing door with my body to pick up Olivia quickly because I wouldn't forgive myself if she was left there, crying and terrified. Our route was easier compared to our route the last time we went to the Philippines, when we had four layovers. This time we only had three— Chicago, South Korea, and Manila.

I knew this trip would be worthwhile because the girls would remember a lot of things. They would also know more people and remember my family and relatives' names. My sisters, Con, Arianne, and Charlotte, would be picking us up again, and I begged them not to be late and make us wait for three hours like the last time because Tim was not coming with us. After a total of twenty-seven hours of traveling— including the layover and one hour delay in Seoul, South Korea—the girls and I were so tired yet happy to meet my sisters at the airport. They were not late, but they went to the wrong airport terminal. Fifteen minutes of waiting was better than three hours. Marie and Olivia were sitting next to Arianne and Charlotte in the taxi cab, and my sisters were amused by talking with the girls and their American accents. They kept giving the girls kisses and hugs. I could tell they missed the girls so much. We were only staying in Manila for a couple days, then we went to Daet, and Arianne went with us.

Daet was booming and different from three years ago. There was a McDonald's downtown, a few restaurants, a new shopping mall, and new businesses—some of them still didn't accept credit cards. The only thing that didn't change was how the people still thought of me because I came from America; I was a walking dollar tree with a lot of money. If they only knew what I did for a living in America—cleaning school and sometimes scrubbing urinals—they would be shocked.

We stayed at Nanay's house, that she was always proud to call her "tiny" home. On the night we arrived, the girls demanded a bath tub, a shower, and an air-conditioned room; unfortunately, Nanay's tiny home didn't have those comforts the girls were looking for. Marie and Olivia started crying when I told them I'd give them a bath using a dipper. Olivia wanted me to show her how I would do that. They told me they wanted to go home and see their daddy after I showed them a big bucket of water and a dipper. Nanay had a big yellow water container, and I dipped water and poured it over their heads. They cried loudly. "It's cold," they whined. I did it quickly, and their crying didn't last long. I didn't want them to sleep at night all sweaty and hot because Nanay didn't have an air conditioner.

Jet lag was hard for the three of us. There were times we slept too early at night and were up at two in the morning. Nanay got up too and started making sunny-side up eggs that Olivia demanded. Then we would talk for an hour or two until we decided to go back to bed again. It only took a day for the girls to show they were really having fun there. They used the restroom by themselves without calling me for help because they were scared. They enjoyed their bath using a dipper; I didn't hear crying anymore, just giggles and laughing. They would say, "It's cold!" Then they would giggle again.

Nanay had no couch; only one foamy "futon," as it's called in America, that became a bed every night. Her television was small with an antenna behind it. "The TV is old," said Nanay. The color changed every time the wind was blowing. The TV screen became red or black, or sometimes the picture couldn't be seen at all; that made the girls complain that they couldn't see anything.

A few mornings, the girls would wake up the same time I did—at five o'clock in the morning—and help me hand wash our clothes that I soaked the night before. They would come out with me to help me hang clothes on the clotheslines. Marie and Olivia spent a lot of time playing hide-and-seek with their cousins, and they always had company to play with. One cousin would come over to the house to play dolls that she brought along with her, and the girls liked that.

I took the girls to the beach; we rode the tricycles (a motorcycle with a sidecar), and walked to see the neighbor's two white goats; the girls said, "They look so cute!" Every morning, I went to the bakery to buy my favorite bread while the girls were still sleeping. Nanay cooked for us, or sometimes we went out to a restaurant.

The girls celebrated their birthdays and they were happy that a lot of kids in the village showed up. I called Tim so that he could greet the girls that day. Marie and Olivia got excited talking to their daddy. I gave them the birthday cards that Tim put in our luggage for their birthdays. They told Tim they missed him so much, and Tim said he missed them too. They were also happy opening presents they got from my family and relatives. They gave away all the pens and the pencils that I picked up from school to their cousins and friends.

We headed back to Manila a few days before our flight to Nebraska because there was one thing I wanted to do before we went back home. I wanted to see my father, who I hadn't seen for twenty-five years, when I was six years old, a first grader, as old as my oldest daughter Marie. My sisters had contact with our brother, Jim, who said our father, Papa, had suffered a stroke. My sisters were coming with me, and we were not going to see him to blame him for whatever he'd done to us. I just want him to see my daughters—his granddaughters, Marie and Olivia— for the first time. I was curious what my father looked like. The only picture I had with him was when Con graduated from kindergarten in Daet where, the three of us—Con, Jim, and I—were standing with Papa in front of a table full of food for Con's simple kindergarten graduation party.

Jim said, "Papa can't sleep well since he found out you are coming to see him. He's been counting the days on the calendar."

He couldn't talk because of his stroke, but he could say three words—one good word and two bad words. But Papa could understand what we said. Walking through the alley reminded me of the kind of life Con and I used to live when I came over to Manila a month after I graduated from college to find a job. My father was living in a slum, and I felt bad for his situation.

I thought there would be tears, long hugs, or asking for forgiveness the moment we saw each other, but none of that happened. No tears flowing down on my cheeks, our arms didn't cross for hugs, and forgiveness wasn't asked when we all met. Papa had a live-in partner who seemed nice and caring, and I was thankful that Papa had someone like her to be with him.

Marie cried a couple times in Daet because she missed her daddy so much, and I would call Tim every other day for fifteen minutes so that he could talk to Marie and calm her down. When I was Marie's age, I never cried because I was missing my father. I only cried because I wished I had a whole family growing up. Looking at Marie, my daughter who'd just turned six years old, I thought how sad it would have been if Tim left us and didn't see his daughters for twenty-five years. But I thought that was impossible and doubtful for Tim to do.

Arianne and Charlotte didn't say much because they couldn't remember anything when Papa left us. Arianne was two years old, and Charlotte was one. Jim and I were old enough and could remember almost everything.

Marie gave Papa a hug, but Olivia didn't want to go to him. "I'm scared," Olivia said to me quietly. She was sitting on my lap, not looking at my father. We took a few pictures with him for me to keep as souvenirs. That was the first picture we had all together, him and his children. I gave Papa a quick hug when we were leaving, and I could see tears filling his eyes. Maybe he wanted us to stay longer, but we had to go.

⌒

Soon enough, we were in the plane, and would be landing in Omaha in an hour. It was a long flight again for the girls, and I just let them sleep on the airplane, watch movies, or color in their coloring books. The girls fell asleep on the chair at the plane gate waiting area; their heads were resting on the big teddy bear that Nanay gave them as a birthday gift. I felt bad looking at Marie's face, covered with small and big red spots. I thought they were from a skin infection she got from Daet. I thought they would hold us at the airport in Manila when the lady pulled us out of the line, and asked if I knew what it was.

"An infection? Allergy? Did she eat anything like a seafood?" the lady asked.

I told her, "It started after we went to the beach, but I'm sure it's not a seafood allergy because Marie didn't eat fish, crabs, or squid when I asked her a couple times. We didn't get a chance to go to a doctor because we're running out of time."

She said okay and let us board the plane. I planned to take her to the doctor once we got to Fremont.

⌣

Marie and Olivia started crying when they saw Tim standing at the airport, holding two red balloons and small gift bags for us. I could tell they missed each other. Tim had to sit down on the bench and had the girls sit on his lap. They told Tim they didn't want to leave him again.

Tim and I decided to take Marie to the urgent care in Fremont to see what was wrong with her face. The doctor diagnosed Marie with impetigo, a bacterial skin infection.

I asked, "How did she get that because I don't think it has something to do with the food she ate."

"Maybe from insect bites," he answered.

I thought he was right. The girls got a lot of mosquito bites when we were in Daet, and Marie's skin got infected because she'd been scratching her legs, arms, and face. The doctor gave Marie a medication and an ointment. "Give these to her for ten days, and her skin infection should be gone in a week. If not, call us," the doctor instructed.

My mind was filled with a lot of things—Tim's new trucking job, my jet lag, Marie's face, and going back to work at the school.

But I didn't want to go back.

My Passion

A few days later, I called Dr. Seaton and gave him my resignation. I told him, "Tim got a trucking job, and there's no way our schedule would work out."

Tim started working at six o'clock in the morning until he got done with his delivery, Monday through Saturday. I stayed home to watch the girls, work with the exchange students, and pursue writing a book.

Dr. Seaton asked if I was interested in working for an after-school program or part-time helping in the kitchen or cleaning. I said no.

"The 'Do What You Love' poster hanging on the wall at the school that I would see every morning when I vacuumed classrooms, is not only for every student to see. It's also for someone like me, a janitor, an immigrant, or someone who has a dream to follow. The only reason we took this job at the school is because it worked out really well for us. I didn't plan to make a career out of it." I told him.

I was thankful that Dr. Seaton understood me, and he wished me luck. "But," he said, "if it doesn't work out, just let me know." I told him I would, even though I was sure I would never call him back to ask for that job.

I remembered during my naturalization ceremony, the judge asked us to look at the big cottonwood tree in the courtyard that was standing so high and strong. The judge said, "It's over a hundred years old, and it witnessed a lot of things that happened in this area. It has a lot of stories," he continued, "just like us, immigrants from all over the world who chose to come over and live in this free country."

In April 2016, I attended a class in Omaha about publishing a book I had written about my work experiences in this country as an immigrant. My first day at work at the school, I picked up fake nails painted silver and orange that were on the floor. And that moment, I thought about my fellow Filipinos who take different, odd, or manuals jobs in a prosperous country like America, disregarding what our friends or families in the Philippines would think and say. They do it because they all want to strive and lift up their families who don't have much in life or live in poverty. That night, I started writing about my job experiences in this country, hoping my writing would someday give ideas to my fellow Filipinos about the hard work and sacrifices that we, the Filipino immigrants, do abroad.

When I submitted that finished manuscript to a book editor, she suggested that I should write more about my immigration journey in this country—the same advice I got from a friend and a stranger.

A few months later, I rewrote that manuscript and I came up with my own journey—this book. I was in high school when I started writing a diary on a spiral notebook. I wrote my dreams—finish college, get a high-paying job someday, drive a car in my twenties, have a family (a daydream of having half-American children), and have a career that I love. I hope I can finish that list in this country by having a career I love. And that's writing.

I called Nanay a day after we got home. Speaking in our dialect, Nanay asked, "How was your flight? How are the girls? I already miss them."

I told her we were all doing fine, except Marie's skin infection. I also told her that I'd just quit my job from the school and that I'd stay home with the girls and finish rewriting my book.

Before we hung up, she told me, in between sniffling "I'm happy for you. Give the girls a kiss and a hug for me." I knew her tears were falling down on her cheeks. And just like when I was entering the NAIA airport gate in Manila last May 2, 2009, with one black suitcase on a sunny Saturday morning to be with Tim, Nanay told me again to "always take care here in Amerika."

Acknowledgments

Writing requires the love for reading, so my deepest gratitude goes first to Mrs. Helen Lumbo, my tutor when I was an elementary student in the Philippines. Thank you for encouraging me to make reading a part of my life.

To our daughters, Marie and Olivia, you're my inspiration for everything I do.

To Mrs. Wava Baylon, I can't thank you enough for all the kindness you showed me when I was in college. I won't forget each moment we laughed together.

To my grandmother, Nanay, who raised me and taught me a lot of things about life. Even though you were strict with us, I appreciate all the values you instilled in my heart and that you taught me to be a responsible person.

I also want to thank my first readers/editors for their insightful comments and suggestions:

Margi McPherson, thank you for reading my first draft. You're a very good friend and an even better critic. You know my story from when I came over to this country, and reaching out to you first was the best step I made after I started writing this. Thank you for being my sounding board too.

Dean Cunningham— As the saying goes, "We can't buy time." Thank you for your time reading my manuscript. Our friendship is our family's treasure.

Jack and Loretta Kloke— Thank you for your honest feedback and making some corrections— grammatically speaking.

Amy Reznicek—I appreciate all your help.

Vicki Sorensen—They say everything happens for a reason, and meeting you brought a lot of reasons for me to be thankful. Thank you for all the ideas, suggestions, and comments about how my book should be.

To Sandra Wendel, thank you for giving me suggestions on how to make this book more interesting.

Although I want to thank some of my nice coworkers from over the years, due to privacy reason I decided not to give names.

To my siblings, my family, and my relatives in the Philippines, thank you for all the support.

To Regina Kodaka, thank you for that small conversation.

To uncle Edwin, who told me we're alike because we're both Sagittarians, we have the same ambitions and we're both dreamers. So, I have to keep dreaming.

To my Filipino friends in Nebraska, thank you for the friendship. My respect to all of you is immeasurable. I've learned so much about your lives and I admire all the hard work you do for yourselves and your families.

To all the Filipino workers around the world, your sacrifices and hard work are something that the world should recognize. I always pray for your safety each day, wherever you are.

My heartfelt thanks to my amazing book editor, Sarah Knight, and the rest of the team at Concierge Marketing Publishing Services.

Finally, I want to thank my supportive husband, Tim, for believing in me since day one of writing this whole manuscript. Also, thank you for being a good father to our daughters. I can't thank you enough.

www.ingramcontent.com/pod-product-compliance
Lightning Source LLC
Chambersburg PA
CBHW031129090426

42738CB00008B/1018